W9-AOR-425

FRONT ROW

SENIOR AUTHOR

Leo Fay

AUTHORS

Barbara D. Stoodt
Dorothy Grant Hennings
Joan M. Baker
Myron L. Coulter

Bilingual Materials
George A. González

The Riverside Publishing Company

Acknowledgments: We wish to thank the following publishers, authors, photographers, illustrators and agents for permission to use and adapt copyrighted materials.

"The Big Orange Splot" is adapted and reprinted by permission of Scholastic Inc. from THE BIG ORANGE SPLOT by Daniel Manus Pinkwater. Copyright ©1977 by Daniel Manus Pinkwater.

"Fiddle-Faddle" in A WORD OR TWO WITH YOU by Eve Merriam. Copyright ©1981 by Eve Merriam. Reprinted with the permission of Atheneum Publishers and of the author. All rights reserved.

"Fly, Jimmy, Fly!" is adapted and reprinted by permission of The Putnam Publishing Group from FLY, JIMMY, FLY! by Walter Dean Myers. Text copyright ©1974 by Walter Dean Myers. Used also by permission of Harriet Wasserman Literary Agency, Inc.

"For a Quick Exit" by Norma Farber first appeared in THE NEW YORK KID'S BOOK, 1967. Reprinted by permission of the author.

"In a Meadow, Two Hares Hide" is adapted from IN A MEADOW, TWO HARES HIDE by Jennifer Bartoli. Text ©1978 by Jennifer Bartoli. Reprinted with the permission of Albert Whitman & Company.

"It's About Time" is adapted from IT'S ABOUT TIME by Miriam Schlein, published by Young Scott Books, A Division of Addison-Wesley Publishing Company, Inc. Copyright 1955 by Miriam Schlein. Used by permission of the author.

"Kate's Secret Riddle Book" is adapted from KATE'S SECRET RIDDLE BOOK by Sid Fleischman. Copyright ©1977 by Sid Fleischman. Used by permission of Franklin Watts, Inc. and Curtis Brown, Ltd.

"Lauren's Secret Ring" is adapted from LAUREN'S SECRET RING by Monica De Bruyn. ©1980 by Monica De Bruyn. Reprinted with the permission of Albert Whitman & Company.

"Mushroom in the Rain" is adapted from MUSHROOM IN THE RAIN by Mirra Ginsburg with permission of Macmillan Publishing Company. Copyright ©1974 by Mirra Ginsburg. Used by permission also of Hamish Hamilton Ltd.

"Nate the Great and the Sticky Case" is adapted from NATE THE GREAT AND THE STICKY CASE by Marjorie Weinman Sharmat. Adaptation reprinted by permission of The Putnam Publishing Group. Text copyright ©1978 by Marjorie Weinman Sharmat. Used by permission also of McIntosh and Otis, Inc.

"Old Blue" is adapted from OLD BLUE by Sibyl Hancock. Adapted by permission of The Putnam Publishing Group. Text copyright © 1980 by Sibyl Hancock.

"On Our Bikes" in THE SIDEWALK RACER AND OTHER POEMS OF SPORTS AND MOTION by Lillian Morrison. Copyright ©1977 by Lillian Morrison. By permission of Lothrop, Lee & Shepard Books (A Division of William Morrow & Co.)

"The Painter and the Bird" is adapted from THE PAINTER AND THE BIRD by Max Velthuijs. ©1971 Nord-Sud Verlag, Switzerland. Published in 1975 by Addison-Wesley, Reading, Massachusetts. Reprinted by permission of Addison-Wesley and Nord-Sud Verlag. "Poem" is reprinted from DIVERSIFICATIONS, Poems, by A. R. Ammons by permission of W. W. Norton & Company, Inc. Copyright ©1975 by A. R. Ammons.

"Seashore Story" is adapted from SEASHORE STORY by Taro Yashima. Copyright ©1967 by Taro Yashima. Reprinted by permission of Viking Penguin Inc.

"The Silver Bay" was originally titled "How the Waters of the Bay Turned Silver" and was first published in KIRIRIKI: STORIES AND POEMS IN ENGLISH AND SPANISH (Houston: University of Houston Arte Publico Press, 1981). Copyright ©1981, 1986 Franklyn Varela-Pérez. Used by permission of Revista Chicano-Riquena.

"Through Grandpa's Eyes" adapted text and eight illustrations from THROUGH GRANDPA'S EYES by Patricia MacLachlan. Pictures by Deborah Ray. Text copyright ©1979 by Patricia MacLachlan. Illustrations copyright ©1980 by Deborah Ray. Reprinted by permission of Harper & Row, Publishers, Inc. and Curtis Brown, Ltd.

ILLUSTRATION: TERESA ANDERKO 125 ALLEN ATKINSON 92–100 YVETTE BANEK 157–167 PENNY CARTER 28–30, 155, 156 NANCY DIDION 246–256 TOM GARCIA 102–110 MARCIA GOLDENBERG 20–25, 27 JOAN GOODMAN 38–47 ANNIE GUSMAN 91, 137, 138–145, 211 MERYL HENDERSON 230–238 DIANE MAGNUSSON 126, 127, 129–135 BEN MAHAN 188–193, 195–202 SAL MURDOCCA 50–60, 245–254, 256 BEVERLY PARDEE 213–218 ED PARKER 79–89 DIANE PATERSON 10–11, 13, 15–18 KAREN PELLATON 111–112, 228–229, 239–243 TOM POWERS 31–37 JAN PYK 70 GRETCHEN SHIELDS 73–78 DOROTHEA SIERRA 154 N. JO SMITH 9, 49, 177 ROBERT STEELE 219–222 SUSAN SWAN 168–175 MOU-SIEN TENG 147–153 GEORGE ULRICH 61, 63–69, 71, 72, 203, 204 FRED WINKOWSKI 205–209

PHOTOGRAPHY: ©BETH BERGMAN 225 TOM ZIMBERRTF/SYMA 226

COVER ART: Tom Powers / Mulvey Associates

Copyright © 1986 by The Riverside Publishing Company.

All Rights Reserved. No part of this work may be reproduced or transmitted in any form or by any means, electronic or mechanical, including photocopying and recording, or by any information storage or retrieval system, except as may be expressly permitted by the 1976 Copyright Act or in writing by the Publisher. Requests for permission should be addressed in writing to: Permissions, The Riverside Publishing Company, 8420 Bryn Mawr Avenue. Chicago, Illinois 60631.

Printed in the U.S.A.

ISBN: 0-8292-4101-9

BCDEFG-VH-898765

CONTENTS

STEP BY STEP 91

WATERWAYS 137

How to Learn New Words

1. Look at the letters in the word.

2. Think of the sound clues.

3. Use the sentence clues.

4. Read the word.

How to Read for Meaning

1. Set a purpose for reading.

2. Think about what you already know.

3. Read the selection.

4. Answer the purpose question.

5. Apply the information.

UNIT 1

REACH FOR THE SKY

LEARN NEW WORDS

1. The birds **flew** from tree to tree.
2. We sat in the **middle** of the boat.
3. She **pretended** to sleep.
4. The bird **soared** higher and higher.
5. She gave the books to her **son**.
6. The **sparrows** went to their nest.
7. They sell apples at the **store**.
8. The plane soared high **above** the trees.
9. He leaned the pole **against** the wall.
10. The people ran down the fire **escapes**.

GET SET TO READ

What would it be like to want something and there is no way to get it?

As you read, see what happens when Jimmy tries to do something he wants very much to do.

Fly, Jimmy, Fly

adapted from a story
by WALTER DEAN MYERS

Two swooping sparrows glided through the air above Jimmy's house. Their shadows slid across the steps where Jimmy sat, and he looked up.

High in the sky, the birds were sailing. Jimmy's eyes followed them. Far above the television antennas, they flew. Way above the clotheslines, they soared. High above the fire escapes, they made looping circles in the sky.

Jimmy wanted to fly, too.

Jimmy's mother called to him. "It's time for lunch, son," she said.

"If I were a bird, I could fly home for lunch," Jimmy thought.

He said, "Mom, can I fly? Birds fly."

His mother smiled and said, "You know you are not a bird and you can't fly."

Each day, Jimmy watched the birds. They flew across the little stamp of sky between the roof tops. They glided like small, playful kites riding a secret wind.

One time, Jimmy stood on the lowest step in front of his house. He reached up high. Then he jumped. He landed on the sidewalk. Jimmy was not happy. He did not wish to jump. He wished to fly.

Jimmy's mother gave him a book about bluebirds, sparrows, and crows. Jimmy found out what crows look like, what sparrows eat, and where bluebirds live. He didn't find out how to fly. Jimmy would have to learn some other way.

Jimmy knew what he would do. He would wait until the birds came closer, and maybe then they could teach him how to fly.

One sunny day, as he sat on the step, a bird swooped down from the sky. The bird came closer. It was chirtering and cheetering. It was telling secrets about flying.

But then a car door closed with a loud bang. "Too loud for the bird," Jimmy thought as he watched the bird fly away.

The next day was sunny, too.

Jimmy sat at his window. He leaned over with his nose against the glass. He sat and he waited and he watched.

Sure enough, some sparrows came. They stopped in the middle of the fire escape. Jimmy thought that now he would learn from the sparrows about flying.

But his mother called, "Come with me to the store, son. We have shopping to do."

On the way to the store, Jimmy thought about the birds. When he got back home, he hurried to the window. But the fire escape was empty. The birds were gone.

Still another time, Jimmy went to see Mrs. Green, who lived on the next block. He heard that she had a bird in a cage. But the bird only sat there like yellow fluff. It sat, pushing against a bell with its beak, but never flying. "Maybe it forgot how to fly," Jimmy thought. "Maybe it even forgot why."

As Jimmy walked home, his mind floated above the sidewalk. He was thinking of the birds. He imagined he could see their shadows. They were flying just above him. Jimmy imagined he was leaping and coming down so slowly, ever so slowly. It was almost like flying.

Back home, Jimmy sat in the middle of the kitchen floor. The sun came through the window, and Jimmy stretched out in the warm circle of sun. The room was full of supper smells. But Jimmy imagined he had left the room. He pretended he was flying. He imagined that he soared above the roof tops and the television antennas. Soon, he was just a speck against the sky.

He stayed in his pretend world until his mother called him for supper. She had hot rolls in her hand. Jimmy imagined swooping quickly down and taking a bite of a roll. Then he imagined that he quickly soared away.

After that, whenever he wanted to fly, he knew what to do. He would close his eyes, tighter than tight. He would picture a sky black as night, with stars to show the way. Then he would pretend to fly.

Over the city and around the moon, he would fly. Over the front steps and around the world, he would fly. Over the lakes and rivers and back home again, he would fly. He would fly. He would fly.

Think About It

1. What different things did Jimmy do when he wanted to learn to fly?
2. How did Jimmy's mother try to help him?
3. How did Jimmy's ideas help him to pretend to fly?
4. What things might Jimmy have seen if he imagined he was flying in the country and not in the city?
5. Write about some things that Jimmy could pretend to do if he wanted to swim like a fish.

LEARN NEW WORDS

1. The books **belong** on this shelf.
2. Of **course** you can have lunch with me!
3. I **finally** got to play.
4. That animal roared like a **lion**.
5. I will help you in a **moment**.
6. Dad **offered** to take us out to lunch.
7. **Perhaps** Sherry is sick.
8. He **refused** to help me with my work.
9. The lost boy had **tears** in his eyes.
10. Her **unhappiness** made me sad, too.
11. Did she **appear** at the back door?
12. We were happy when the dancer **arrived**.
13. I will **either** go or stay.

GET SET TO READ

If a pet were lost, how would it get home?
Read to see how a bird gets home.

THE PAINTER AND THE BIRD

adapted from a story
by MAX VELTHUIJS

Once there was a painter. But because he could not sell his paintings, he was not very rich. He had painted many beautiful pictures. He loved all of his paintings, but he had one favorite. It was a picture of a strange and wonderful bird.

One day, a man arrived at the studio to look at the painter's pictures. He looked at all of them for a long time and saw one picture that he liked best of all. It was the painting of the strange and wonderful bird.

Of course, the painter refused to sell that painting, but the man would have no other. The man finally offered to put the painting in a very special place. The painter could no longer refuse. He wanted the painting of the wonderful bird to be in a special place, so he decided to sell the painting.

The man took the painting of the bird to his big house in the country. He hung it on the wall of his favorite room. There, he could always enjoy his new painting.

But the strange and wonderful picture bird was filled with unhappiness! He missed the painter who had painted him.

And so, one day . . . the picture bird flew away.

The picture bird flew into a barnyard, where he met a rooster. "Perhaps you can tell me where to find the painter who painted me," said the picture bird. "He is a kind man and has a bushy, red beard."

"Oh, I can't," said the rooster. "I don't know anyone with a beard. I never leave this barnyard. Go and ask the birds in the forest. They fly everywhere. Perhaps they can help you."

The picture bird flew a long way and finally arrived in the forest. The birds in the forest laughed at the picture bird. "You really are a strange-looking bird," they said. When he asked if they could tell him where to find the painter with a bushy beard, the birds in the forest said, "Why don't you try the zoo? There is someone there with a beard. Perhaps he is the one you are looking for."

So the picture bird flew off to the zoo. Soon he found someone with a beard. But it was a lion, not a painter.

"If you sit on my head, you will look like a crown," said the lion. "Nothing would make a more beautiful picture than a lion with a crown on its head. Perhaps your painter will come and offer to paint my picture."

So the picture bird stayed in the zoo. Many people came to see the lion with the strange and wonderful bird sitting on its head like a crown. "Perhaps the painter does not know I am here," said the picture bird. So he flew away to find his friend.

The sad picture bird flew and flew, crying tears of unhappiness.

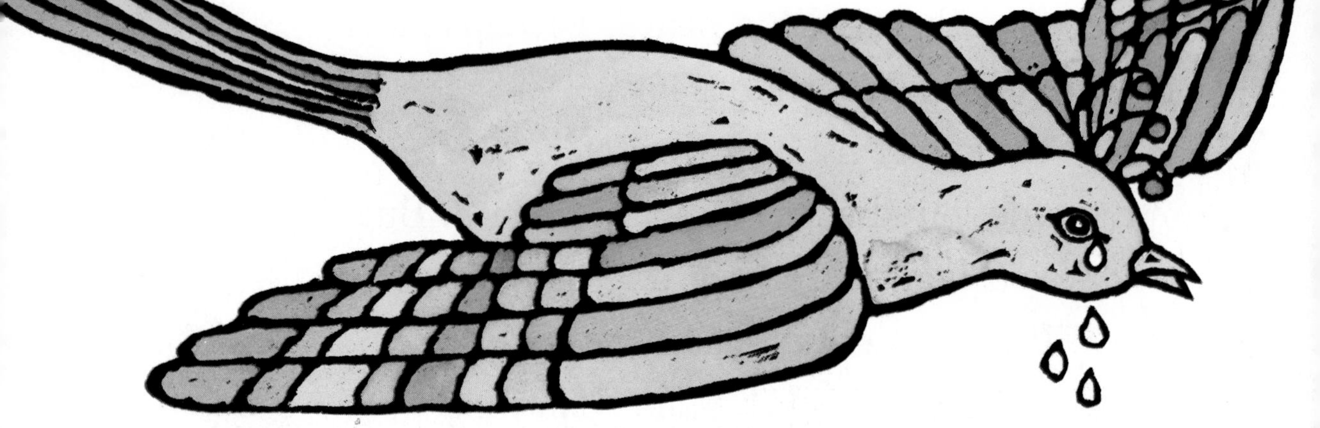

Then he saw something flying against the sky that looked like a huge white bird. The picture bird thought, "Perhaps it can help me." But the huge white bird flew much too fast, until finally it was so far above him that the picture bird could not see it anymore.

Soon the picture bird grew tired. He flew down to a field. He was all alone. He cried tears of unhappiness once more.

At that moment, a boy and a cat came by. The boy listened to the bird's story, and suddenly the boy remembered that he had seen the picture bird before.

"I know where you belong," the boy cried. "I know where your friend the painter lives. Come with me!"

So off the three of them went to find the painter's studio.

At that very moment, who should appear at the painter's studio but the man who had bought the painting! He had the picture under his arm and was very angry. He wanted the bird back.

"You sold me a picture of a bird, but there is no bird in the picture!" said the man. "Either give me my money back, or repaint a bird in this picture!"

The painter refused to repaint the bird, so he gave the money to the man. The man gave the picture back to the painter. So now the painter had no money and no bird either.

The moment the man left, the boy, the cat, and the picture bird appeared at the back door. The painter's eyes were filled with tears of joy. Of course, the picture bird was happy, too, and flew right back to where he belonged in the picture.

The painter promised to refuse to sell the painting ever again. The bird promised never to fly away again.

And so the two friends lived together happily for the rest of their lives.

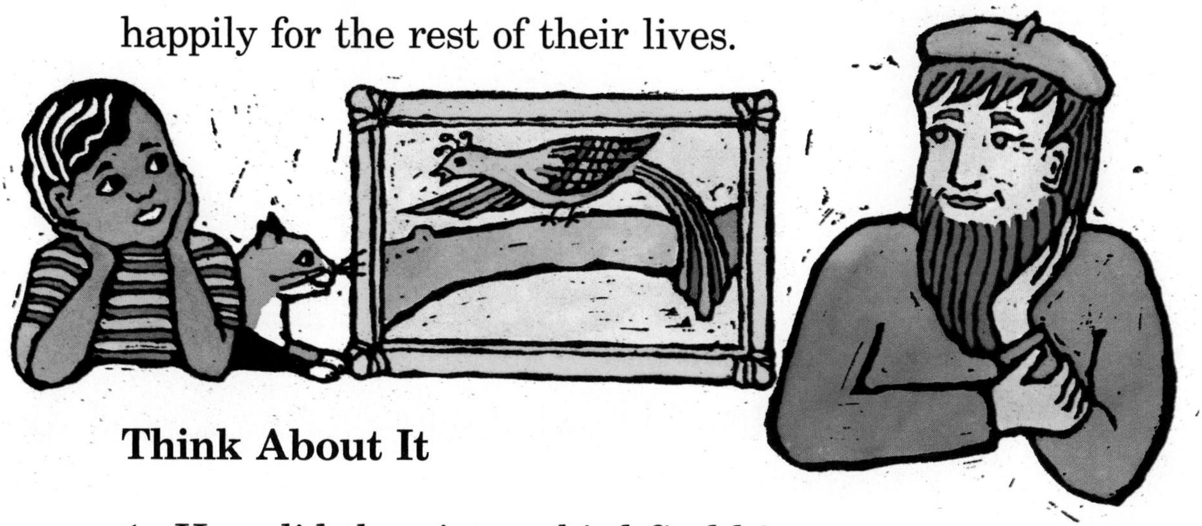

Think About It

1. How did the picture bird find his way home?
2. How did the lion help the picture bird?
3. How did the boy help the picture bird get home?
4. How is the picture bird different from the birds in "Fly, Jimmy, Fly"?
5. What would your own special picture bird look like? Draw a picture or write a story about your picture bird.

POEM

by A. R. AMMONS

In a high wind the
leaves don't
fall but fly
straight out of the
tree like birds

How Things Are the Same and Different

In "The Painter and the Bird," the rooster said, "I never leave this barnyard." He told the picture bird to go to the birds in the forest. "They fly everywhere," he said.

How was the rooster different from the birds in the forest?

The rooster could have said, "I never leave the barnyard, but the birds in the forest fly everywhere." The word *but* would show that he was going to tell how the other birds were different.

Many things are the same in some ways. But they are different, too.

When you see two things together, you can tell how they are alike and how they are different. Look at the two newspaper ads. How are they alike? How are they different?

SAVE MONEY
ON
FAT-TIRE BIKES
THIS WEEK ONLY
$20.00 OFF
EVERY BIKE
HAND BRAKES, STREAMERS, BELLS
COME IN TODAY
GRADY'S BIKE SHOP
410 HARRIS ST. 475-6500

GIANT BIKE SALE

Our sale is for this week only.
Every bike in the store is on sale.
Come in today.

Rosa's Bikeland

LEARN NEW WORDS

1. We finally **began** to eat our lunch.
2. They **built** a cage for the rabbit.
3. Dad **depends** on me to watch Tina.
4. Some plants need **direct** sunlight to live.
5. The rain fell **during** lunch.
6. The sun gives us clean, safe **energy.**
7. Our dog just **lies** around all day.
8. There are **millions** of stars in the sky.
9. What kind of **power** makes a car run?
10. We can use **solar** energy to keep warm.
11. Our stove works with **electricity**.
12. Will we need cars in the **future**?
13. The space **station** needs sunlight.

GET SET TO READ

Did you know that sunlight is energy? Read to find out about ways the sun's energy is used.

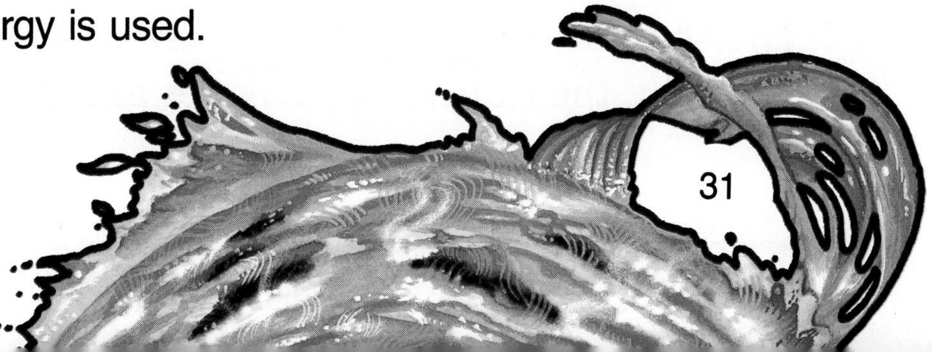

Sun Power

by DUNCAN SEARL

As long as the sun is shining, this toy train goes around and around. The train depends on sunlight to make it run. During the day, the little power station next to the tracks must "reach for the sky" and turn sunlight into electricity to make the train run. When the sun goes down at night, the train loses its power and stops.

Power from the sun is called *solar energy*. You can do an experiment to show that the sun gives energy. Place a jar of cold water next to a sunny window. Let some time go by, and then put your fingers in the jar. The water will feel warmer. It has been heated by energy from the sun.

Solar energy is used in many ways. A cat that lies in a sunny window depends on solar energy. When you walk on the sunny side of the street, you are using solar energy to keep warm.

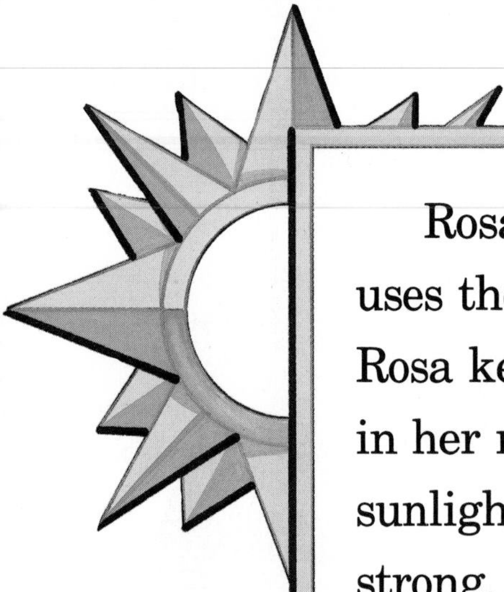

Rosa is using solar energy, too. She uses the sun's energy to grow vegetables. Rosa keeps her plants in a sunny window in her room. She depends on direct sunlight to make the plants grow tall and strong. Without the sun, it would be very hard to grow food.

Did you ever hear someone say, "It is so hot, you could cook your food on the sidewalk"?

That is a funny way to speak about using solar energy. But some people have built stoves that *do* cook by using sun power. On a hot day, the rays of the sun heat the stove. Of course, the stove must be near a window that lets in the sun. Just think! You can cook dinner and be warmed by the sun at the same time!

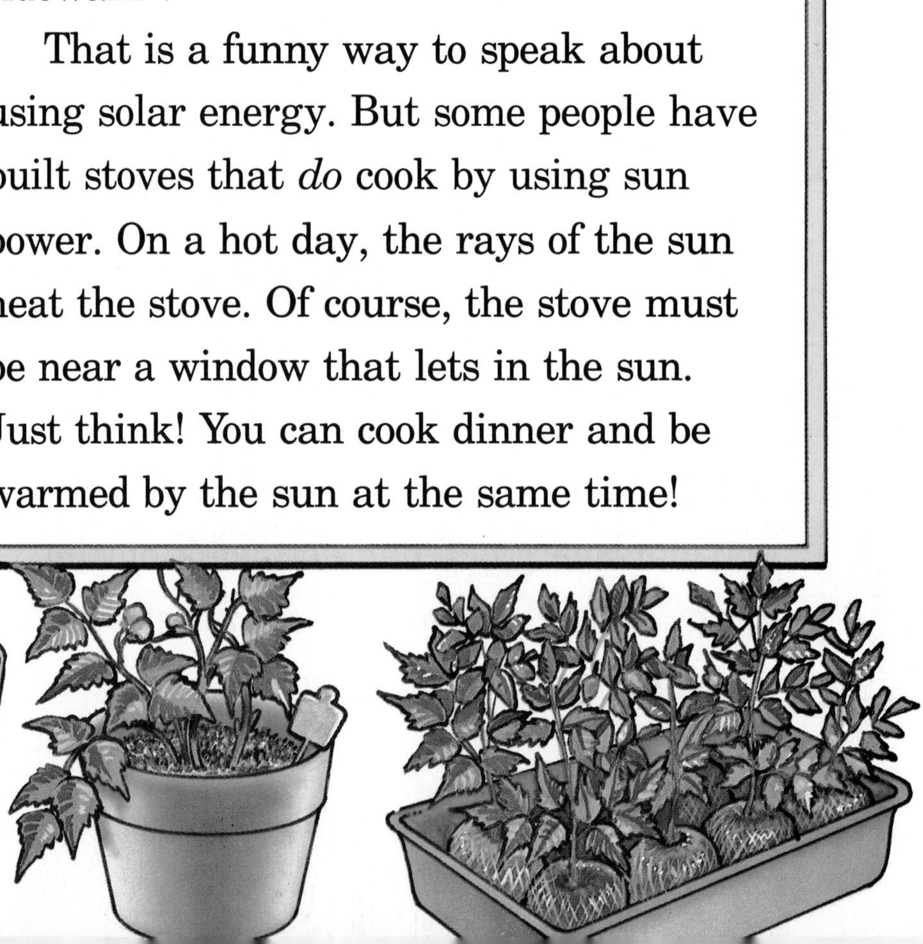

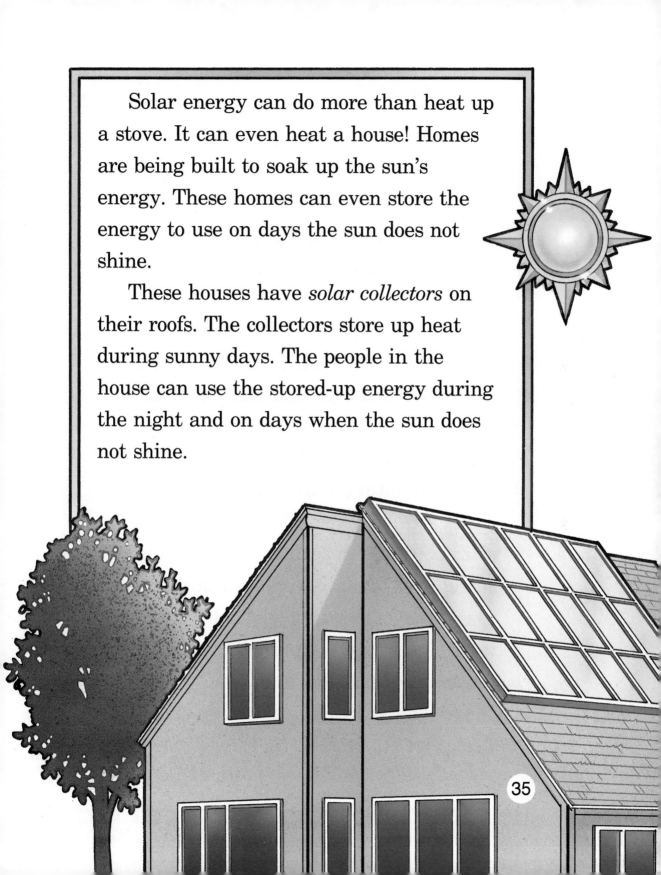

Solar energy can do more than heat up a stove. It can even heat a house! Homes are being built to soak up the sun's energy. These homes can even store the energy to use on days the sun does not shine.

These houses have *solar collectors* on their roofs. The collectors store up heat during sunny days. The people in the house can use the stored-up energy during the night and on days when the sun does not shine.

When you began to read this story, you learned about a small solar-power station that can make enough electricity to power a toy train. There is a giant solar station in France. It lies in direct sunlight and has rows and rows and still more rows of solar collectors. This power station uses direct sunlight to make electricity, too. But it can make enough electricity for a whole town! In the future, we are likely to see many solar-power stations like this one.

In the future, other uses for solar power will be found. Right now, we use solar power for space travel. When space travel first began, no one was sure if a spaceship could stay in space for a long time. The machines and lights on a spaceship use up lots and lots of power. Where do you think a spaceship gets all of that power?

The answer is solar energy. Today's spaceships make their own electricity from sunlight. Using energy from the sun, a spaceship could travel millions and millions of miles through space!

The sun has always given us energy. To use this energy, we all must try to "reach for the sky."

Think About It

1. What are some ways solar energy is used?
2. How can solar energy be used even if the sun is not out?
3. How can solar energy help us in space?
4. What does "reach for the sky" mean in this story?
5. Write about the ways you might use solar energy in the future.

Lauren's Secret Ring

adapted from a story
by MONICA DE BRUYN

Lauren was new in town. She didn't have any friends, but she had a special secret. She owned a magic ring.

One day when Lauren was giving bits of food to the birds in the park, she had seen the ring shining on the ground.

"Maybe someone left it here just for me," she thought. Then she slipped the ring on her finger.

Lauren had always been good at pretending. But after she found the ring, she was even better at it.

On her way home, she heard the birds up in the trees. "I wonder what they are singing about today," she said.

Lauren held the ring up and watched it shine against the sunlight. Suddenly, she knew. The birds were talking about her!

"See! See! See!" called the sparrows. "The ring! The ring!"

"She has it! She has it!" cried a bluebird.

A big old crow flew down next to Lauren. "Can I have it? Can I have it?" he asked. Lauren refused the selfish crow. "Not for anything in the world!" she said.

In the morning, Lauren kept the ring on when she went to school.

Lauren was lonely, walking so far with no one to talk to. "I wish I could go very fast. Then school wouldn't seem so far away," Lauren thought, turning the ring on her finger.

And suddenly, she seemed to be floating. But no one knew she was floating—except Lauren. After that, Lauren put the ring on every day before she went to school.

She didn't worry anymore about knowing the right answers for her new teacher. When she touched the ring, she could think of just what to say.

And when it was time to go to the playground, Lauren was alone. Then she touched her ring and listened to the birds talk. She stood in the playground and thought, "I can wait to make friends."

Sometimes, she would stop to see Sharkey, the big dog that lived in a doghouse built next to the school. By touching her ring, Lauren could understand everything he said.

Sharkey was tired of sitting alone in his yard. With the help of her ring, Lauren told him beautiful stories.

Lauren's pets at home liked her to touch the ring and tell stories, too.

"I will make new friends soon," Lauren often thought. "For now, I have my pets and my ring."

Then one awful morning, her ring was gone! She looked everywhere for it.

"Well, I just won't get up," Lauren decided, getting back into bed. "I won't do anything today either."

But Lauren's mother had a different idea. "It is time to get up," she said with a smile. "You will feel fine at school, and perhaps you will make a new friend."

Lauren groaned, but she pushed herself out of bed.

It took her a long time to dress that morning. And when Lauren tried to eat, the food seemed to stick in her mouth.

Without her ring, Lauren couldn't float. It seemed to take a long, long time to walk to school.

All morning, she sat very still. "What if the teacher calls on me, now that my ring is gone?" she thought.

Suddenly, the room was quiet. "Lauren," her teacher was saying, "I asked you what six and three is."

Lauren jumped. "Oh!" she said. She thought. "Is it nine?"

Lauren's teacher smiled. "Very good."

Lauren didn't know how she had thought of the right answer without her ring.

Soon it was time for the lunch bell.

Lauren sat down at the lunch table, feeling very bad. She remembered that she had not brought her lunch.

"What is it, Lauren?" asked a girl named Sue.

"I forgot my lunch," Lauren said.

"Well, here, taste this piece of chicken," Sue offered. "I have two pieces."

Just then some other children came by.

Julia offered Lauren an orange. Danny gave her some carrot sticks. Jerry gave her an apple. Lauren was surprised. It felt like a party!

After lunch, Lauren took the children to the school yard to meet Sharkey.

"Won't he hurt us?" asked Jerry.

"Oh, no, he just wants a story," Lauren told him.

"Tell him a funny story," said Sue, "and see if he laughs."

"Well, I can try," Lauren said. But she didn't know if she could, without her ring.

She started a silly story about a doghouse. As she talked, Sharkey sat very still. He seemed to smile. Lauren could tell that this was the best story she had ever made up.

In the middle of the story, the children heard the school bell ring. It was time to go back to class.

After school, Lauren saw Sue again.

"Where do you live?" asked Sue.

"On River Street," said Lauren.

"Why, so do I! Why don't you come over to see the box my brother and I built for the toad we found?"

"Let me tell my mother, and then I can come," said Lauren shyly.

When Lauren got home, there was her ring on the middle of the kitchen table.

"I found the ring this morning," said her mother. "I thought it might be your favorite ring."

Lauren just stared, and then she smiled.

She picked up her ring and put it away in her special box.

"I think I can give it a rest for a while," she said.

READ ON!

Ellsworth and the Cats from Mars by Patience Brewster. Ellsworth has a strange dream that comes true.

A Child's Book of Birds by Kathleen Daly. Read this book to learn interesting facts about birds.

Little Pieces of the West Wind by Christian Garrison. A farmer loses some socks. Read to find out what happens when the West Wind tries to get them back.

Follow the Wind by Alvin Tresselt. Can anyone stop the wind? Where does it go? Read to find out.

The Emperor and the Kite by Jane Yolen. Read how a young girl uses a kite to save her father.

UNIT 2

Little Riddles

LEARN NEW WORDS

1. My **blanket** keeps me warm.
2. Did the dog **chew** on an old shoe?
3. A **clue** helps you find the answer.
4. The baby was **extra** quiet today.
5. Don't stand **near** the water.
6. The rain made **puddles** in the street.
7. Do you want to hear a funny **riddle**?
8. The **sign** says that the store is open.
9. I keep my **slippers** under my bed.
10. Annie has a hard problem to **solve**.
11. I **swapped** my extra pencil for a pen.
12. Is she **able** to solve the riddle?
13. They will arrive at five **o'clock**.

GET SET TO READ

How do you try to find something lost? As you read, see what Nate the Great does to find a missing stamp.

Nate the Great and the Sticky Case

adapted from a story
by MARJORIE WEINMAN SHARMAT

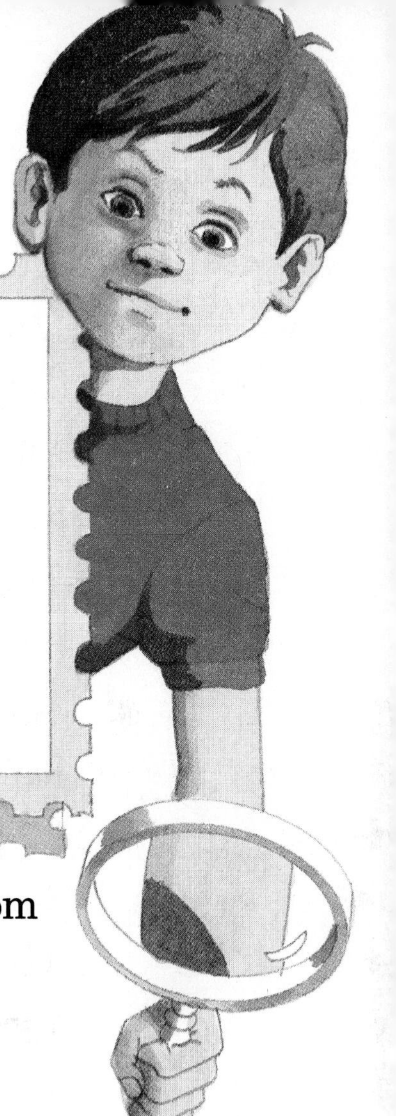

I, Nate the Great, was drying off from the rain. I was sitting under a blanket and reading a detective book. My dog Sludge was sniffing it.

I was on page 33 when I heard someone knock on the door. When I opened it, Claude was there, and he looked very unhappy. "I lost my prize dinosaur," Claude complained. He was always losing things.

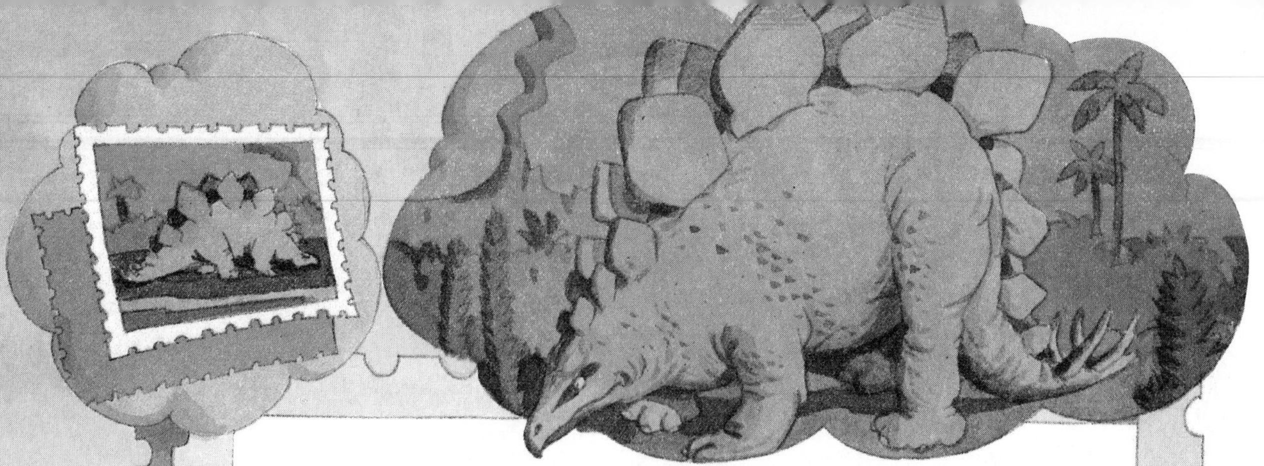

"This is your biggest loss yet," I said. "A dinosaur is huge."

"*My* dinosaur is small," Claude said. "It is a picture of a stegosaurus on a stamp. I hope you can help me find it."

"This will be a big case to solve," I said. "But I'll take it, and I hope I will be able to solve it. Tell me, where was the stegosaurus stamp the last time you saw it?"

"It was on a table in my house," Claude said. "I was showing all my dinosaur stamps to my friends."

"Who are your friends?" I asked.

"Annie, Pip, Rosamond, and you. But you were not there," Claude added.

"I, Nate the Great, will go to your house and look at your table," I said.

So I threw off my blanket. Then my dog Sludge and I went with Claude to his house. He showed me his table, which had rows of stamps all over it. "Here are all my stamps," Claude said, "except for the stegosaurus stamp."

"Where was the stegosaurus stamp when it was on the table?" I asked.

"Near the edge," said Claude.

"It must have fallen off," I said. I looked on the floor near the table. The stegosaurus stamp was not there. I picked up a stamp and showed it to Sludge.

"We must find a lost stamp," I told him. Sometimes, Sludge is not a great detective. But at other times, he is. This time, Sludge tried to lick the sticky side of the stamp. "*Look*. Don't lick," I said.

I looked all around Claude's house. We did not find his prize stegosaurus stamp.

"Tell me, when did you find out the stamp was missing?" I asked.

"After everyone left," Claude said.

"Did everyone leave together?" I asked.

"Yes," said Claude.

"Did everyone come together?" I asked.

"No," said Claude. "Annie and Rosamond came at about two o'clock to tell me that Rosamond was going to have a yard sale. Then it started to rain. It rained for a long time. So Annie and Rosamond stayed and looked at my stamps.

"When the rain stopped at three o'clock, Pip came over. He looked at my stamps, too. Then they all left together to go to Rosamond's yard sale."

Sludge and I went to Rosamond's house. In front, an extra-large sign said "Yard Sale." Rosamond was selling rows and rows of pink feathers, empty tuna fish cans, bicycle parts, paper crowns, and other kinds of things.

"Do you have any stegosaurus stamps for sale?" I asked Rosamond.

"No," said Rosamond, "but there was one at Claude's. He just loves dinosaurs."

"Thank you," I said.

Then I saw Pip looking at some slippers. "Did you see Claude's stegosaurus stamp?"

Pip doesn't say much. He just shook his head up and down. "Do you know where it is now?" I asked. Pip shook his head from side to side. "Thanks," I said.

Next, I saw Annie and her dog Fang. "What do you know about Claude's stamp?" I asked.

"I know that the stegosaurus is pretty," Annie said. "It looks like Fang. Show us your stegosaurus smile, Fang," she said.

Fang opened his mouth. It looked as if he had a million teeth! I, Nate the Great, knew it was time to go home.

At home, I wrote notes in my notebook on everything I knew about the case so far. I wrote that it was not raining when Annie and Rosamond went to Claude's house and saw the stamp near the edge of the table. Then, while they were at Claude's house, it rained for a long time. But when Pip went to Claude's house, the rain had stopped.

Raindrops were on the trees. Puddles were on the sidewalk. I, Nate the Great, thought of Pip stepping in the puddles.

I got a stamp from my desk and put it on the floor. Then I went outside. The signs of the rain were all gone, except for some puddles. I stepped in one of the puddles to get my feet wet. Then I went back inside and stepped on the sticky side of the stamp. The stamp stuck to my shoe!

The same thing must have happened to the stegosaurus stamp and Pip's shoe at Claude's house.

I remembered that Sludge had tried to lick the sticky side of the stamp. That would have made the stamp very sticky and a sticky stamp . . . sticks! Suddenly I knew that Sludge *was* a great detective after all. He had given me the clue I needed to solve the riddle of this sticky case.

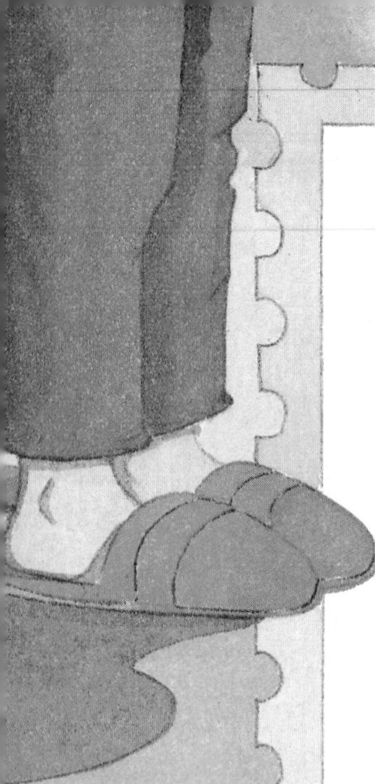

Now I knew I had to see Pip's shoes. I called Sludge, and we ran over to Pip's house. When Pip opened the door, I looked down at his feet. He had on some slippers. "Where are your shoes, Pip?" I asked.

"My shoes were all wet from the rain," said Pip. "After I left Claude's house, I swapped them for some slippers at Rosamond's sale and put my shoes in their place."

"Thank you," I said, and Sludge and I went back to Rosamond's sale. We looked at the swap table, but Pip's shoes weren't there.

"I want Pip's shoes," I told Rosamond.

"I just sold them to Annie for a dime," Rosamond said. "It was my biggest sale."

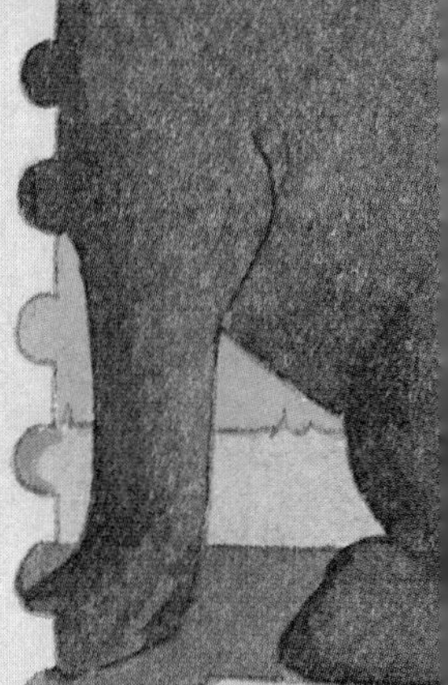

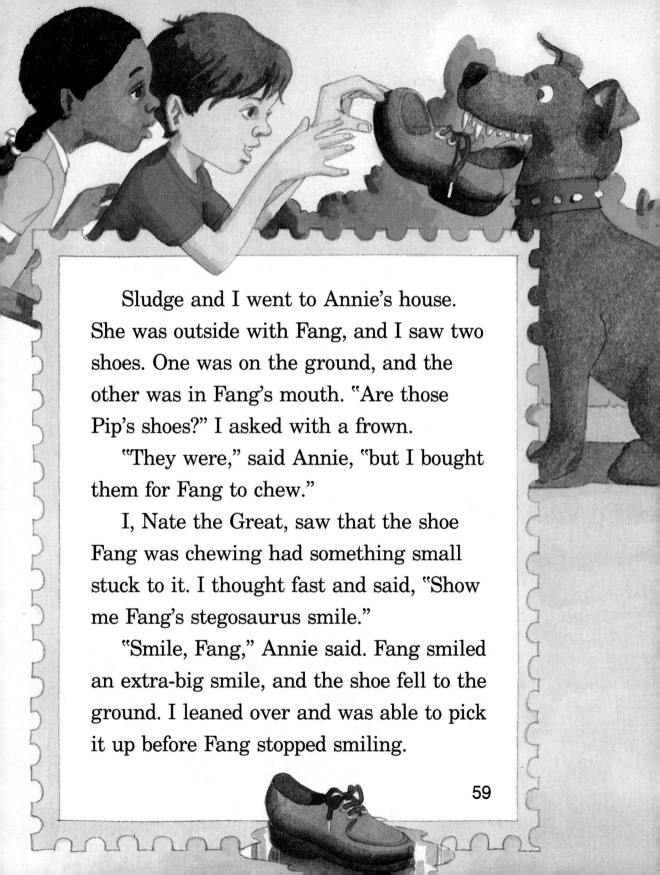

Sludge and I went to Annie's house. She was outside with Fang, and I saw two shoes. One was on the ground, and the other was in Fang's mouth. "Are those Pip's shoes?" I asked with a frown.

"They were," said Annie, "but I bought them for Fang to chew."

I, Nate the Great, saw that the shoe Fang was chewing had something small stuck to it. I thought fast and said, "Show me Fang's stegosaurus smile."

"Smile, Fang," Annie said. Fang smiled an extra-big smile, and the shoe fell to the ground. I leaned over and was able to pick it up before Fang stopped smiling.

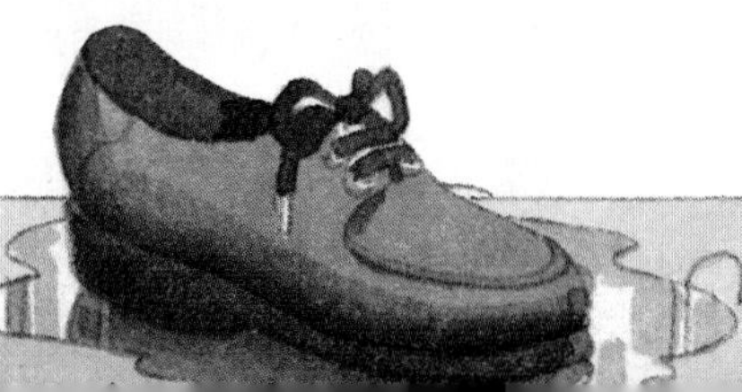

I, Nate the Great, pulled off the stamp. The riddle of the missing stegosaurus stamp was solved. Sludge and I took the stamp to Claude's house. Claude was very glad to get it back.

Think About It

1. What different things did Nate the Great do to solve the case?
2. How did knowing that Pip went to Claude's house *after* it had rained help Nate solve the case?
3. How did Sludge help Nate?
4. How is playing detective like solving a riddle?
5. Think of a place in the classroom to hide a ball. Write clues to show how to find the ball. Ask a friend to name the hiding place.

LEARN NEW WORDS

1. They are **burning** oak logs.
2. Do you like **butter** on your vegetables?
3. Please bring me a **full** glass of milk.
4. She left this **message** for you.
5. Write the **numerals** *5* and *2* on the box.
6. How many extra **sentences** did you write?
7. Five riddles were **written** on the page.
8. She was **awake** when I left.

GET SET TO READ

How would you send a message that no one but your friends could understand?

Read on to learn some secret codes.

It's a Secret

by BERTHA RADER

Beverly had to send a secret message to her friend Joe. She had to let him know their club's new password.

Beverly sent the message in code. A *code* is a secret language. Beverly's code was easy for Joe to read. She used an alphabet shift code. The full code looked like this.

A	**B**	**C**	**D**	**E**	**F**	
C	D	E	F	G	H	
G	**H**	**I**	**J**	**K**	**L**	**M**
I	J	K	L	M	N	O
N	**O**	**P**	**Q**	**R**	**S**	
P	Q	R	S	T	U	
T	**U**	**V**	**W**	**X**	**Y**	**Z**
V	W	X	Y	Z	A	B

This message is written in Beverly's shift code. Can you read it?

Yjgtg ctg vjg ugetgv rncpu?

(Turn the book upside down for answer.)

In this code, Beverly would write the word *clue* as if it were spelled *enwg*. The new password was *melted butter*. In code, that is spelled *ognvgf dwvvgt*.

Beverly wrote Joe about the new password. The next day, the club had its meeting. Joe whispered "Melted butter" at the clubhouse door. He had no problem getting into the meeting.

Answer: Where are the secret plans?

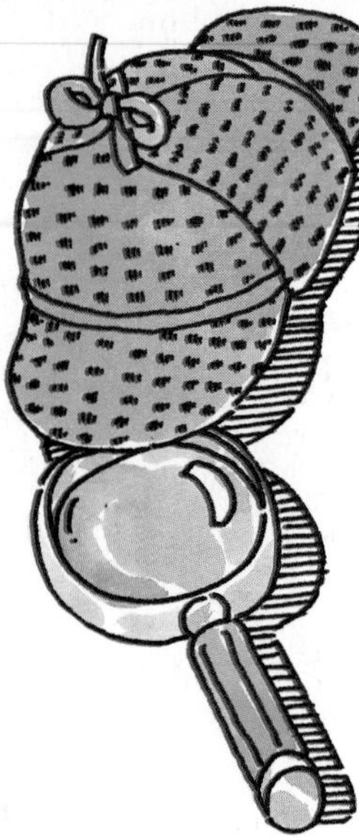

Joe's favorite code uses numerals. In his code, each letter of the alphabet is replaced by a numeral. *A* is the first letter of the alphabet, so its code numeral is *1*. *B*'s numeral is *2*, and so on up to *Z*'s numeral, which is *26*. Here is Joe's favorite numeral code.

A 1	**B** 2	**C** 3	**D** 4	**E** 5	**F** 6	
G 7	**H** 8	**I** 9	**J** 10	**K** 11	**L** 12	**M** 13
N 14	**O** 15	**P** 16	**Q** 17	**R** 18	**S** 19	
T 20	**U** 21	**V** 22	**W** 23	**X** 24	**Y** 25	**Z** 26

When Joe sends a numeral code message, he puts a dash between the numerals. That helps make the code easy to read.

Use Joe's numeral code as a clue, and read this message.

1. 9 8–9–4 20–8–5 6–15–15–4 9–14 20–8–9–19 19–1–3–11.

Now put this message into a numeral code.

2. Meet me under the blue light bulb.

(Turn the book upside down for answers.)

Answers: **1.** I hid the food in this sack.
2. 13–5–5–20 13–5
21–14–4–5–18
20–8–5 2–12–21–5
12–9–7–8–20 2–21–12–2.

The codes you know will help you answer these riddles.

The answers to the first two riddles are written in the alphabet shift code. Can you find the answers?

1. Which is heavier, a pound of rocks or a pound of feathers?
Vjga gcej ygkij c rqwpf.

2. What has a face but can't talk?
C enqem qt c ycvej.

(Turn the book upside down for answers.)

Answers: **1.** They each weigh a pound.
2. A clock or a watch.

The answers to the next two riddles are written in the numeral code. Can you find the answers?

3. What is heavy and light at the same time?

1 7–9–1–14–20 12–9–7–8–20 2–21–12–2.

4. What can a runner put on to listen to music while running?

1 8–5–1–4–2–1–14–4.

(Turn the book upside down for answers.)

Answers: **3.** A giant light bulb.
4. A headband.

Some codes do not give a message letter by letter. These codes use words to stand for other words, for sentences, or for whole messages.

Beverly and Joe like to talk in word codes because they are harder for other people to solve. Only people with a code key can solve the code. Any words can be used in a code. *Butter* could mean "Call me up." *Swap* could mean "after school." *The stew is burning* might mean "Meet at our clubhouse." *Awake* might mean "Hello."

There can be millions of codes. You can find out about them from books, or you can make up your own. When you use a code, always make sure that your friends have the right key for solving it. If anyone else solves your code, change it! That way your secrets will stay secret.

Think About It

1. What kinds of secret codes did you learn from this story?
2. How can you use numerals in a code?
3. What do you need to solve a word code?
4. Tell how a detective like Nate the Great might use a code to solve a case.
5. Try making up your own letter code, a word code, or any other kind you like. Then write a message in your code, and ask your friends to "crack the code."

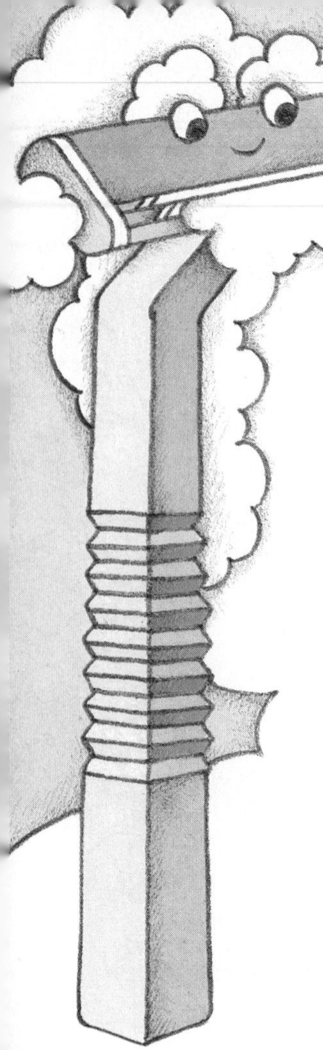

Fiddle-Faddle

by EVE MERRIAM

Riddle me no,
riddle me yes,
what is the secret of Success?

Said the razor, "Be keen."
"String along," said the bean.
"Push," said the door.
"Be polished," said the floor.
Said the piano, "Be upright and grand."
"Be on the watch," said the second hand.
"Cool," said the ice cube.
"Bright," said the TV tube.

Working Out Word Riddles

Some words are like little riddles. They can trick you because they have more than one meaning. Look at these two sentences.

1. Beverly sent a **letter** to Joe.
2. Beverly shifted **letter** *a* to letter *b* to start her code.

What meaning does the word **letter** have in the first sentence? What meaning does it have in the sentence after that?

Sometimes, you may not be sure of the meaning of a word. Use the other words in the sentence as a sign or clue to help you know the meaning.

Dear Beverly,
I'm writing this letter to tell you about the new code. The letter C stands for the letter A and the letter D stands for the letter B.
Get it?

These sentences are part of the directions for playing a game. Look at the sentences. Choose the right meaning for each underlined word.

1. Turn around and **stamp** on the grass.
   a. something you use to mail a letter
   b. step hard
2. **Roll** the ball across the floor.
   a. move by turning over and over
   b. a kind of food
3. **Rock** your body in time to the music.
   a. a kind of stone
   b. move from side to side
4. Do not **lean** on the little tree or it will break.
   a. put your weight against
   b. thin
5. Read the note on the **slip** of paper.
   a. move suddenly without wanting to
   b. a small piece

LEARN NEW WORDS

1. A rock fell to the **bottom** of the sea.
2. She was able to throw **farther** than I.
3. Does it **matter** if I sit in the third row?
4. He dropped a **pebble** into the puddle.
5. A **single** blanket isn't warm enough.
6. I need **strength** to carry the box.
7. The **thirsty** horse ran to drink the water.

GET SET TO READ

Imagine that you have to reach something on a very high shelf. How would you try to reach it?

As you read, see what Crow does to get something she can't reach.

The Crow and the Water Jug

an AESOP fable adapted
by ROSEANN FRANCIS

One day, a thirsty crow found a jug with some water at the bottom of it. "How lucky I am!" thought Crow. "Now I can have a drink of water." She bent her head and put her beak into the jug. But the water was so low in the jug that Crow's beak could not reach it.

So Crow bent over a little farther. She still could not reach the water. She bent over even farther. She stretched her neck and flapped her wings. But still she could not get a single drop of water to drink.

Then Crow decided to try to make the jug lie on its side. "This will make the water run out of the jug. Then I will be able to drink from it," she thought. She pushed at the jug with all her strength. But no matter how hard she tried, the jug did not fall over. And the water stayed at the bottom of the jug, too low for Crow to reach.

"I may as well give up," Crow thought. She was very thirsty and very tired. She would have flown away to look for water right then. But suddenly she had an idea.

Crow scratched in the dirt until she dug up a pebble. She dropped the pebble into the jug. She could see that the pebble made the water a little higher. So she scratched for another pebble and another and another. She dropped every single pebble that she could find into the jug. As each pebble went in, the water rose a little bit higher. At last, the jug held many pebbles. The water had reached the top of the jug.

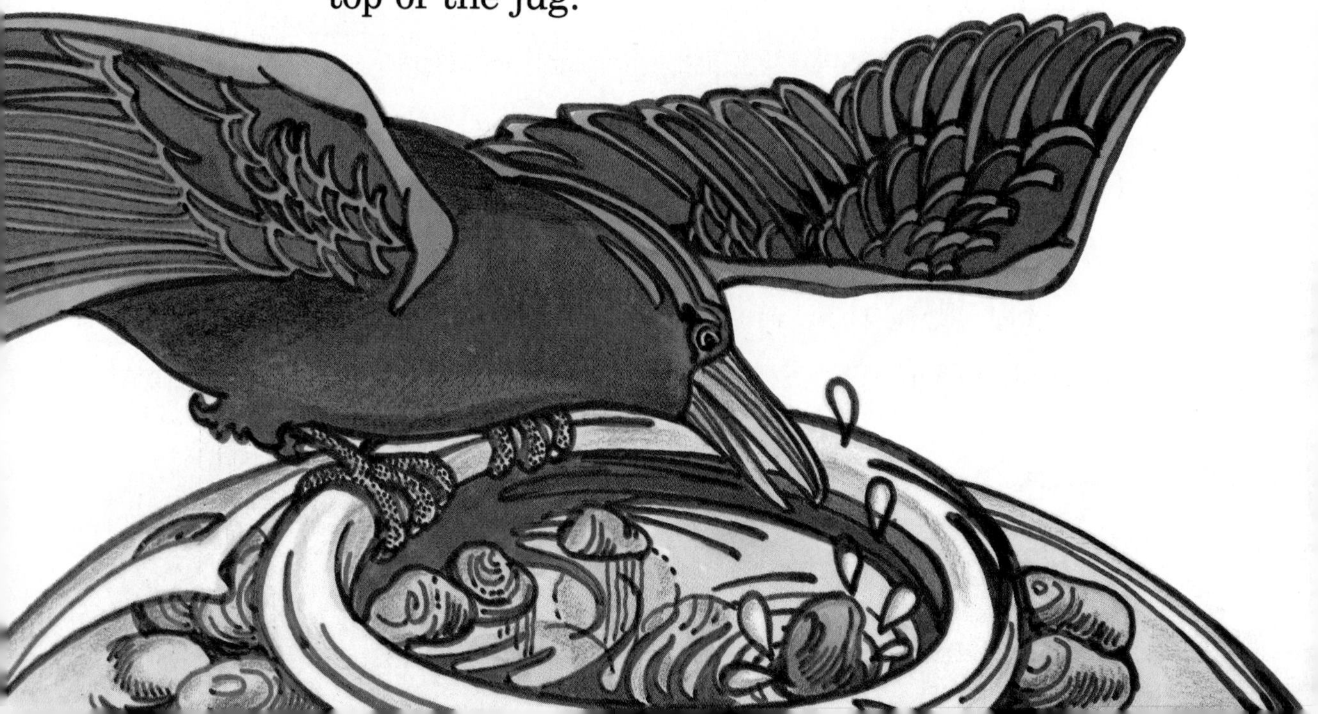

"Caw, caw!" Crow said. "I did it!" The water rose to the top of the jug. Crow took a drink out of the jug.

"I could have flown away without getting a drink," she thought. "I am so glad I found a way to reach the water."

Crow thought she wasn't strong enough to get at the water. But she learned that strength doesn't always matter. Sometimes, the only thing on which you need to depend is good thinking.

Crow flapped her wings and flew away. She wasn't thirsty any longer.

Think About It

1. Why can't Crow get a drink of water?
2. What were the different ways that Crow tried to reach the water?
3. What did Crow *finally* do to get a drink of water?
4. How do you think that what Crow did is like solving a secret riddle?
5. Tell how Crow could have gotten a drink of water if she had not found the jug.

KATE'S SECRET RIDDLE BOOK

adapted from a story
by SID FLEISCHMAN

I hope you don't have a friend like Wally. Wally lives directly across the street. He is always playing silly tricks, and then he laughs and waves his arms up and down like a huge chicken.

One day, Wally knocked at our door and said to me, "Let me in, Jimmy."

"No," I answered, "my sister Kate is sick."

"I want to tell her a riddle," said Wally. "It will make her laugh."

I hadn't found a way to cheer up Kate all week, so I let Wally in.

"Do you want to hear a riddle?" Wally asked my sister.

"No," said Kate.

"It's a funny riddle," Wally smiled.

"Well, all right," Kate said.

"Here's the riddle," said Wally. "Watchdog!"

"That's not a riddle!" I said.

"It's the answer to one," Wally said. "You have to think of the question." He was laughing so hard he almost fell over.

Then Wally waved his arms up and down like a chicken. He laughed all the way out of the house.

"I feel sick," Kate said.

"You were already sick," I said.

"Well, I feel sicker than before," Kate said. "Wally will never tell us the first half of the riddle."

"Maybe someone else knows it," I said. "I'll try to find out. See you later."

As I left the house, I saw the man who lives next door.

"Do you know any riddles, Mr. Rivera?" I asked.

Mr. Rivera thought for a moment. Then he said, "Pretend that I am a fly. What would I say if I had flown into soft melted butter?"

"Watchdog?" I asked.

"No," said Mr. Rivera. "Look! I am a butterfly."

At the vegetable store near my house, I asked Mrs. Mitchell, "Do you know any riddles?"

"Let me think," she said. "If I were a lamp, what would I say to another lamp?"

"Watchdog?" I asked.

"No," said Mrs. Mitchell. "Got any bright ideas?"

As I helped Mr. Levy carry his bundles out to his car, I asked, "Do you know any riddles?"

"Of course I do," said Mr. Levy. "If you put a clock in the woods, what time would it be?"

I couldn't solve that one either, so I said, "I give up."

"Why, it would be tree o'clock!" Mr. Levy said with a smile.

Mr. Levy was the third one I asked. I still didn't know the answer to Wally's riddle, so I walked down the street for a while, thinking hard. Maybe Wally had made up that silly answer. That gave me a bright idea.

I ran back to the store and bought a small notebook. I decided to write down all the riddles I knew before I forgot about them.

I stopped to write them in the book, and on the cover I wrote

What did the crow say after eating Mrs. Smith's blackberries?

"Thank you berry much!"

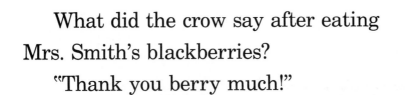

How did three goldfish walk across the street?

Don't be silly. Goldfish can't walk.

When can it rain pennies?

When there is some change in the weather.

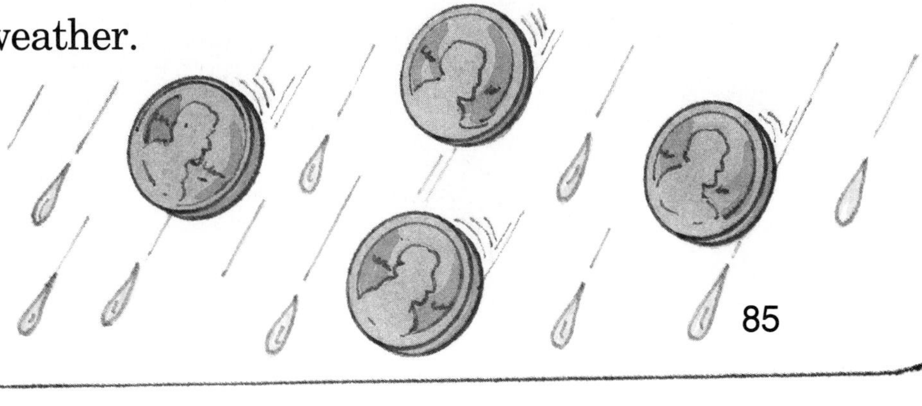

Just then, something happened across the street. Mr. Cross's dog ran into the yard. Mr. Cross looked at his watch and shouted, "Good dog! You're on time for dinner!"

All at once, I yelled, "That's it! If *watchdog* is the last half of Wally's riddle, then I know the first half!"

I wrote my idea in the book and ran home as fast as I could. I gave the riddle book to Kate.

Before long, my sister Kate and I were laughing so hard that Wally could hear us from across the street. He came over to our house and asked, "What are you laughing at?"

"We are laughing at the first half of your riddle," Kate answered.

I said, "Wally, that's the funniest riddle in the whole world."

"It is?" asked Wally.

"I can't stop laughing," said Kate.

Then Wally said, "Tell me the first half of the riddle. Tell me!" he said again and again.

"But you know it," said Kate.

"No, I don't," said Wally. "The fact is, I just made up that answer to trick you. I don't know the question."

"You are just saying that," Kate laughed. "It's so funny. But don't worry. My brother Jimmy and I promise to keep your prize riddle a secret, no matter what."

"Please tell me," Wally said.

"Do I hear your mother calling you?" asked Kate. "You had better go home."

Then Kate picked up her book and looked at the last riddle again. Here is what she read:

What kind of animal keeps time best?
Watchdog
(Don't tell Wally.)

READ ON!

Snow Is Falling by Franklyn M. Branley. Read this book to find out all about snow.

How Many Kids Are Hiding on My Block? by Jean Merrill and Frances Gruse Scott. Ten children hide. All but one are found. Where is the last child?

Crickets and Frogs, a Fable in Spanish and English by Gabriela Mistral. Read all about Old Cricket and his song.

Hey Riddle Diddle! by Rodney Peppé. The pictures in this book will help you answer the riddles.

Detective Mole and the Secret Clues by Robert Quackenbush. Find out how Detective Mole opens some doors.

UNIT 3

STEP BY STEP

LEARN NEW WORDS

1. I like the **autumn** season best.
2. The station is just **beyond** that hill.
3. We could not see in the **darkness**.
4. The **eagle** flew to the edge of the nest.
5. She ran to the **safety** of her home.
6. The turkey ran **straight** into the barn.
7. We **swept** away the snow with a brush.
8. The **young** child began to cry.
9. The hare raced **ahead** of the toad.
10. What is that walking **toward** me?

GET SET TO READ

Think of what you would do if a friend suddenly needed help.

As you read, see what Mimo does to save Lepo.

In a Meadow, Two Hares Hide

adapted from a story
by JENNIFER BARTOLI

In a meadow, it was morning. The tall grass shone in the early sun. A young hare hopped about the field. Her name was Mimo. She was hungry and thirsty, and it was time to look for food.

Here, she found the last of the summer's wild grapes, which were wet and sweet. Mimo chewed many of the grapes. Then she crouched in the darkness of the bushes and watched the meadow around her.

Down a small grassy hill, Mimo saw a shadow move toward her. She sat up, ready to leap away as she sniffed the air and looked again.

Coming toward her was Lepo, a young hare who was all brown and white and furry.

Deep in the sunny grass, the two hares looked at each other. Lepo put out a paw, and Mimo's long ears went straight back.

But suddenly, Mimo's ears were up again. She sniffed the cool wind. Then she leaped into the air.

Lepo also heard something and turned toward the woods. There, only the tips of two pointed ears showed beyond the grass.

A fox had come into the meadow. When the fox saw Mimo and Lepo, the chase was on. The two young hares ran, turning and darting to escape the fox. Their two white tails bobbed up and down in the grass. The fox was close behind.

Mimo could feel the fox behind her. It was coming nearer and nearer. Ahead, she saw a thicket of sharp branches hanging low over the grass. She raced under them to safety.

The fox was fast, but so was Mimo.

Once more, the meadow was quiet. One dark eye peeked out from the thicket. Mimo was safe now, and the fox had gone.

But where was Lepo? Mimo sniffed the autumn air and then listened for him. The grass was still. She could not smell him. Mimo was alone.

Slowly, the warm days of autumn ended. Leaves died, and winter came to the meadow. Mimo's fur grew thick to keep her warm. It was white now and matched the snow. Only the tips of her ears were dark.

Mimo was always hungry, but she looked for food only at night or in the safe darkness of early morning. When light filled the sky, Mimo hid in the safety of her home in the snow.

Early one morning, Mimo came to a path of new tracks on top of the snow. She raised her ears and listened to the wind as it swept up the snow. Then she touched the tracks with her nose.

These were Lepo's tracks—she could tell. Directly ahead stood a line of trees. Lepo had gone around them. Mimo could see more of his tracks ahead.

Mimo followed the tracks. She hopped around the trees, too.

Beyond the trees, Lepo was looking for food in the snowy field. Suddenly, an eagle screeched as it flew across the morning sky. Lepo heard it and looked up with excited eyes.

The eagle saw him. Where could Lepo go? Lepo turned so that the sun and the screeching eagle were behind him. He raced zigzag across the meadow. The snow sprayed up in the air and made a fine white path where Lepo ran.

The eagle swept closer.

Suddenly, out jumped Mimo! The eagle and the hares screeched in the cold, quiet air. Mimo threw out her strong back legs and swept the eagle to the ground. The eagle slipped, its sharp claws digging into the snow.

This was their chance to run to safety. Mimo and Lepo ran.

The eagle was up quickly. It screeched as it flew in great circles over the meadow, but already Lepo and Mimo were too far ahead and beyond its reach.

The two hares ran until they came to lie in some tall green grass growing in the snow. Here was food for them and a place to hide.

And here Mimo and Lepo could rest at last. Now they were both safe.

Think About It

1. What did Mimo do to help save her friend Lepo?
2. How did sniffing the air or the wind help the hares protect themselves?
3. How was the meadow different in autumn from the way it was in winter?
4. Tell how Lepo and Mimo became friends "step by step."
5. Some animals change color when they need to protect themselves. In what ways do people make sure they are protected in different kinds of weather?

LEARN NEW WORDS

1. When he was **done** eating, he left.
2. The ride took so long it seemed **endless**.
3. It is one **minute** closer to lunch.
4. Autumn won't be here for many **months**.
5. She walked a **quarter** of a mile.
6. We floated across the **river**.
7. I solved that riddle in ten **seconds**.
8. The lake is **sixty** miles long.
9. How do you **suppose** he made that sign?
10. Wally left at **exactly** six o'clock.
11. The party began exactly one **hour** ago.
12. My sister is **twelve** years old.

GET SET TO READ

We can't see or touch time. Yet we need it.

Read to find out what people mean when they talk about time.

It's About Time

adapted from a book
by MIRIAM SCHLEIN

Tick, tock, tick, tock! Hear the ticking of the clock! Time is going by. Where is it going? Can you see it passing by?

People say, "Time flies"—but can you see it flying through the air? Where has it flown?

Everyone says, "It is a long time." Is time like a long, long piece of string on a kite?

Sometimes, someone says, "Take your time." Can you take a supply of time with you in a box?

What do people mean when they talk about *time*?

Time can be a quarter of an hour, a bit of a day, or a week, or a year.

It is here. Then it is gone forever.

Time is—plip!—as quick as it takes you to wink your eye.

And time is all the days you must wait until next summer comes.

People have given names to bits of time as they pass. There are always sixty seconds in one minute. There are always sixty minutes in one hour. There are always twenty-four hours in one day. Every year has twelve months in it. Just think of how many seconds it takes to make one year!

Tick, tock, tick, tock. You can never stop time or make it go faster or slower.

Then why do people always want to know *exactly* what time it is?

Sometimes, you really *have* to know exactly what time it is.

If you are not on time, you might miss the party. If you are late, the train will leave without you, or you'll miss the first part of the circus.

Tick, tock, tick, tock. Ready, set, go, or you'll be late!

Suppose the circus starts at exactly ten o'clock. How do you know when it's ten o'clock?

It's easy. Just look at the clock. When the short hand points to the ten and the long hand points straight up to the top—to the twelve—it is exactly ten o'clock.

Everything that happens, happens in a space of time.

At the circus, the dog climbs up and rides the horse, and the elephants dance. Suddenly and quietly, time has swept by.

Look! The long hand on the clock has moved past fifteen dots. It points to the three. The short hand still points to the ten. Fifteen minutes have passed—one quarter of an hour. It is a quarter past ten.

Time always keeps moving ahead. Even when nothing is happening, time keeps passing. It flows on and on. It never stops.

Your clock can stop, but time never stops. It is endless.

Look! The long minute hand has moved some more, and five more minutes have passed.

Tick, tock, tick, tock. You are five minutes older!

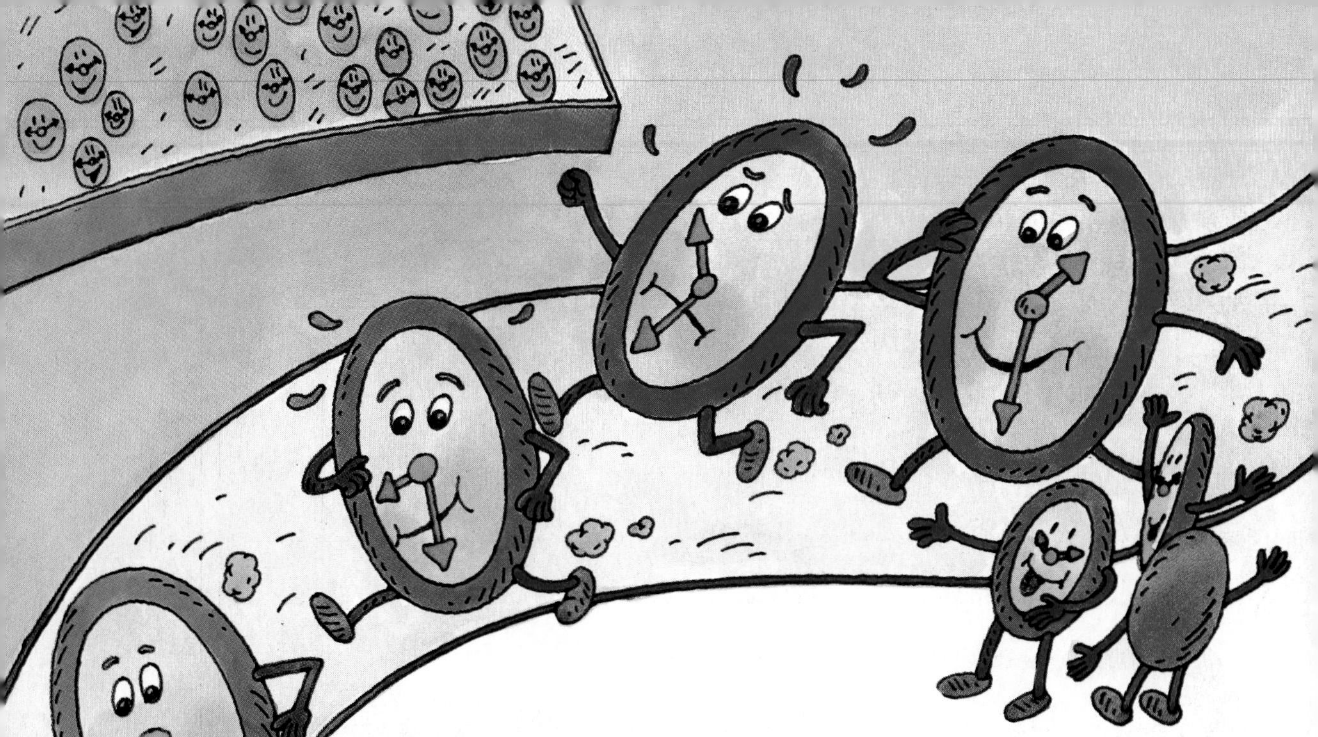

Time always keeps going by. Each hour is always sixty minutes. It is never any more or less. Sometimes, it may *seem* like more.

If you are waiting for something special to be done, an hour can seem very long. It can seem endless.

But suppose you are having fun. An hour seems to pass, whsst, just like a minute!

But it's not a minute. It's an hour—and that is always sixty minutes.

But time is not just told by a clock.

Time goes by in the woods and the fields. You know that animals do not have clocks hanging in the trees. How do you suppose they know when day is done?

They don't know the words *night* and *day*. But they see it get dark. And they know the day is through. They know the night is about to begin.

Time goes by for the animals, too.

Time goes by for everyone. Twelve months or sixty seconds go by for a king with his crown or a bee or a fish in the sea. Time goes by for you and for me. We all share time as it passes.

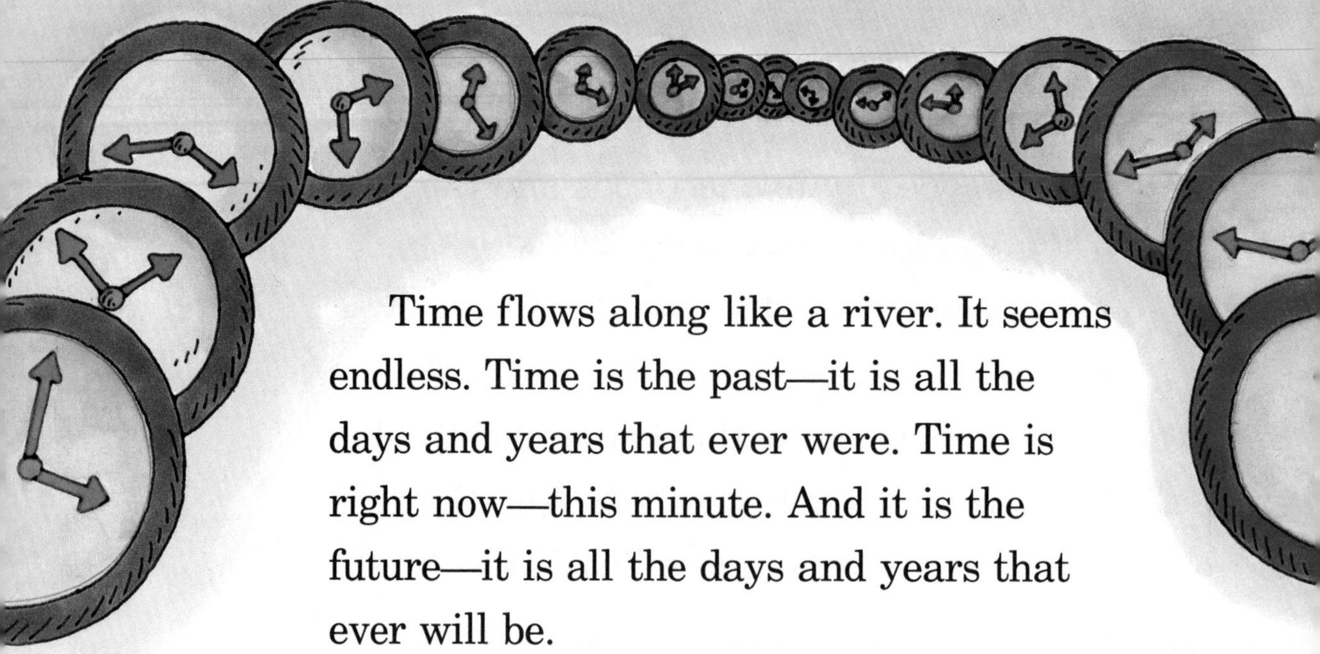

Time flows along like a river. It seems endless. Time is the past—it is all the days and years that ever were. Time is right now—this minute. And it is the future—it is all the days and years that ever will be.

Think About it

1. What do people mean when they talk about time?
2. What would happen if you did *not* know how to tell time?
3. What might happen if you arrived someplace too late?
4. How do you think the hares in the last story could tell that time was passing?
5. Tell why on some days you need to know how to tell the exact time.

SKILLS

Taking Steps in Time

Everything you do happens in time. You open your eyes and get dressed in the morning. Then you do many other things. At night, you sleep.

When you read, you see clues that tell you at what time things are happening. What *time* clues do these sentences have?

a. At a quarter past twelve, the dog chews the bone and then chases its shadow.

b. Seconds before dinner, the butter burned in the pan.

Now use the *time* clues to answer the questions.

1. When does the dog chew the bone and chase its shadow?

2. When did the butter burn?

When you learn about science, you find that things happen at different times. What *time* clues do these sentences have?

a. Most birds sleep at night.
b. The bat sleeps during the day.
c. Some birds fly south in winter.
d. Many birds build their nests in spring.
e. Young birds are hungry during the day.
f. After about three weeks a baby chicken leaves its shell.

Now use the *time* clues to answer the questions below.

1. When do most birds sleep?
2. When does the bat sleep?
3. When do some birds fly south?
4. When do many birds build nests?
5. When are young birds hungry?
6. When does a baby chicken leave its shell?

LEARN NEW WORDS

1. We had eggs for **breakfast**.
2. We played a game of **dominoes** after lunch.
3. To keep up your strength, do **exercises**.
4. Please put the box down **gently**.
5. **I'm** surprised that he is not awake.
6. He **tunes** his banjo before playing it.
7. He plays beautiful tunes on his **cello**.

GET SET TO READ

What does it mean to look at something "through someone else's eyes"?

Read to find out what John does to "see" things the way his grandfather does.

Through Grandpa's Eyes

adapted from a story by PATRICIA MACLACHLAN

Of all the houses that I know, I like my Grandpa's best. Grandpa's house is my favorite because I see it through Grandpa's eyes. Grandpa is blind. He doesn't see the house the way I do. He has his own way of seeing.

In the morning, the sun pushes through the curtains into my eyes. I dig down into the blankets to get away, but the light follows me. I give up, throw back the covers, and run to Grandpa's room.

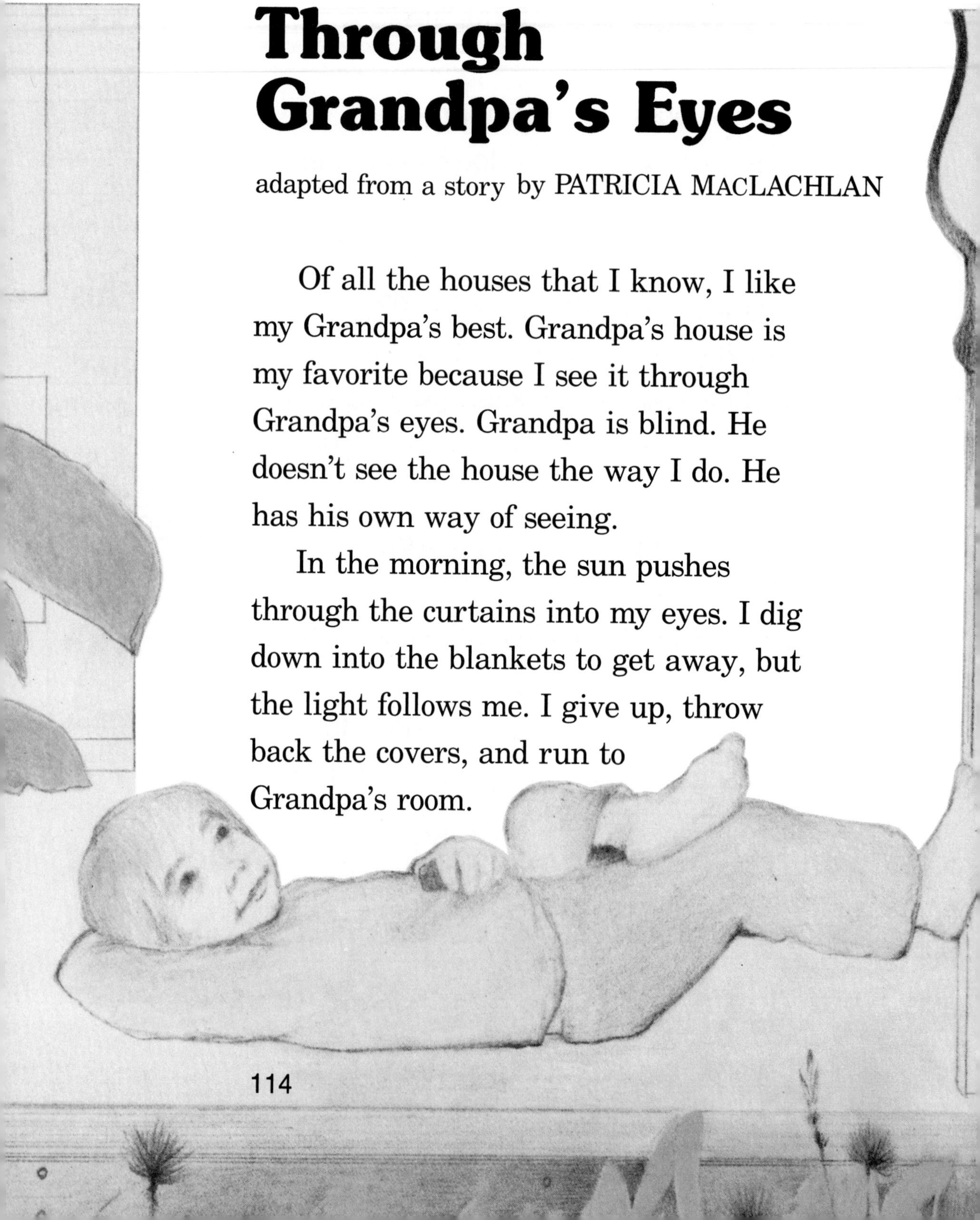

The sun wakes Grandpa differently. He says it touches him, *warming* him awake. When I peek around the door, Grandpa is already doing his exercises.

"Good morning, John," Grandpa says.

"Where is Nana?" I ask him.

"Don't you know?" he says. "Close your eyes, John, and look through my eyes."

I close my eyes. Downstairs, I hear the banging of pots and the sound of running water that I didn't hear before.

"Nana is in the kitchen making breakfast," I say.

I exercise with Grandpa, up and down, up and down. When I try to exercise with my eyes closed, I fall. Grandpa laughs gently when he hears me thump on the floor.

"Breakfast!" Nana calls up.

The wooden banister at the stairs is smooth from Grandpa running his fingers up and down. I imitate him, my fingers following his smooth path.

We go into the kitchen and say "good morning" to Nana.

"Close your eyes, John," Nana says, "and tell me what breakfast is."

"I smell eggs and toast," I say.

"You are getting to be just as good as Grandpa," Nana says with a smile.

We all sit down at the breakfast table. When Grandpa eats, the food on his plate is placed like numerals on a clock.

"Two eggs are at eight o'clock, and toast is at two o'clock," says Nana to Grandpa.

I make my plate like a clock, too, and eat my food as Grandpa does.

After breakfast, I follow Grandpa to the living room. He opens the window to feel the weather outside. His cello is in the corner of the room.

"Will you play your cello with me, John?" he asks.

He tunes our cellos without looking. I place my music on a stand before me. For a minute, I close my eyes and play through Grandpa's eyes. My fingers move up and down the cello neck. Because I cannot see, my bow falls from the strings.

"Listen," says Grandpa, picking up his bow. "I will play some music I learned when I was your age."

He plays the music, and I listen so I will learn the way Grandpa learns. First, he listens; then he plays the music.

"Now," says Grandpa, "let's play it together."

"That is fine," says Grandpa as we play a tune. "You are good."

Later, Nana brings out her clay. She is making a clay model of Grandpa's face.

"Sit still," she grumbles with a smile.

"I won't," he says, imitating her grumbly voice and making us laugh.

When Nana is finished, Grandpa runs his hand over the clay head. His soft fingers move quickly and gently.

"It looks like me," he says, surprised.

My eyes have already told me that it looks like Grandpa. But he shows me how to use my fingers to feel his own face and then the clay face.

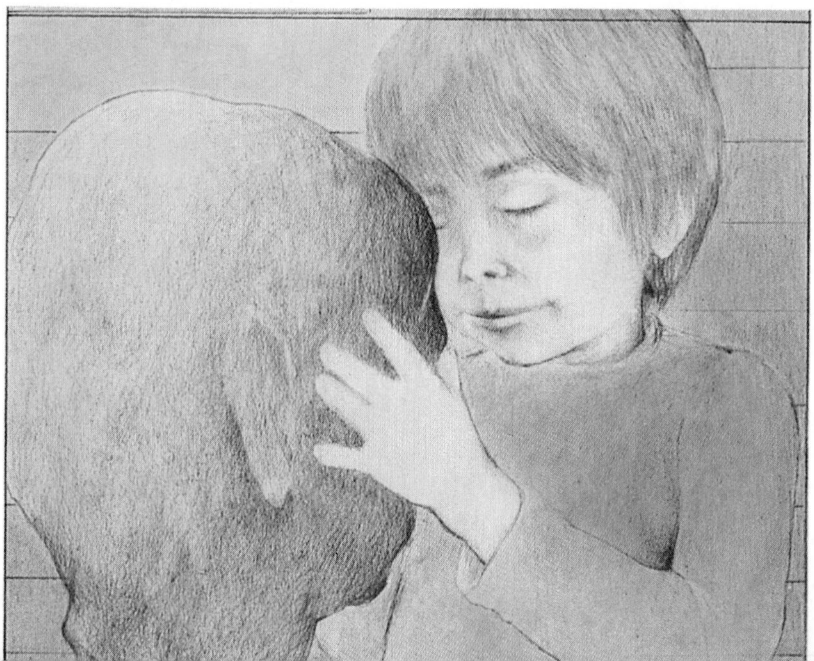

"Pretend your fingers are water," he tells me.

I try to imitate the way Grandpa uses his fingers. I let my waterfall fingers flow over the clay head, filling in the spaces under the eyes before they flow softly over the cheeks. The clay face feels like Grandpa. This time, my fingers tell me.

Later, Grandpa and I walk outside and across the field to the river. This is Grandpa's favorite place. Grandpa has not always been blind. He remembers seeing the sunlight on the river and the trees in the forest. But he gently takes my arm as we walk. We go step by step.

Near the river, a bird calls to us. It is black with a red patch on its wing. Without thinking, I point my finger at the bird.

"What is that bird?" I ask excitedly.

"A red-winged blackbird," says Grandpa.

He can't see my pointing finger, but he hears the music of the bird.

As we walk back to the house, Grandpa stops suddenly.

"Honkers," he whispers.

I look up and see geese high in the sky, flying like a big *V*.

"Canada geese," I tell him.

"Honkers," he says again, and we both laugh.

After lunch, Grandpa, Nana, and I take our books outside to read under the apple tree. Grandpa reads his book with his fingers, feeling the raised Braille dots that tell him the words. As he reads, Grandpa laughs out loud.

"Tell us what's so funny," says Nana.

So Grandpa reads to us.

After supper, Grandpa turns on the television. Nana and I watch, but Grandpa listens, and the music and words tell him when something is scary or funny, happy or sad.

Later, we play dominoes. Grandpa carefully feels the white dots on each domino and wins the game.

Somehow, Grandpa always knows when it is bedtime. I say "good night" to Nana. Then he takes me up and helps me get ready for bed.

As Grandpa leaves my room, he says "good night." But before he leaves, he pulls the light chain above my bed to turn out the light. But, by mistake, he has turned it on instead. I lie for a minute before I get up to turn off the light. I lie in the darkness, smiling at his mistake.

Then, when there is darkness for me the way there is darkness for Grandpa, I hear the night sounds that Grandpa hears. I can hear the clock ticking downstairs, the birds singing their last songs of the day, and the wind moving through the trees outside my window.

Suddenly, I hear the sounds of geese. They are flying low over the house.

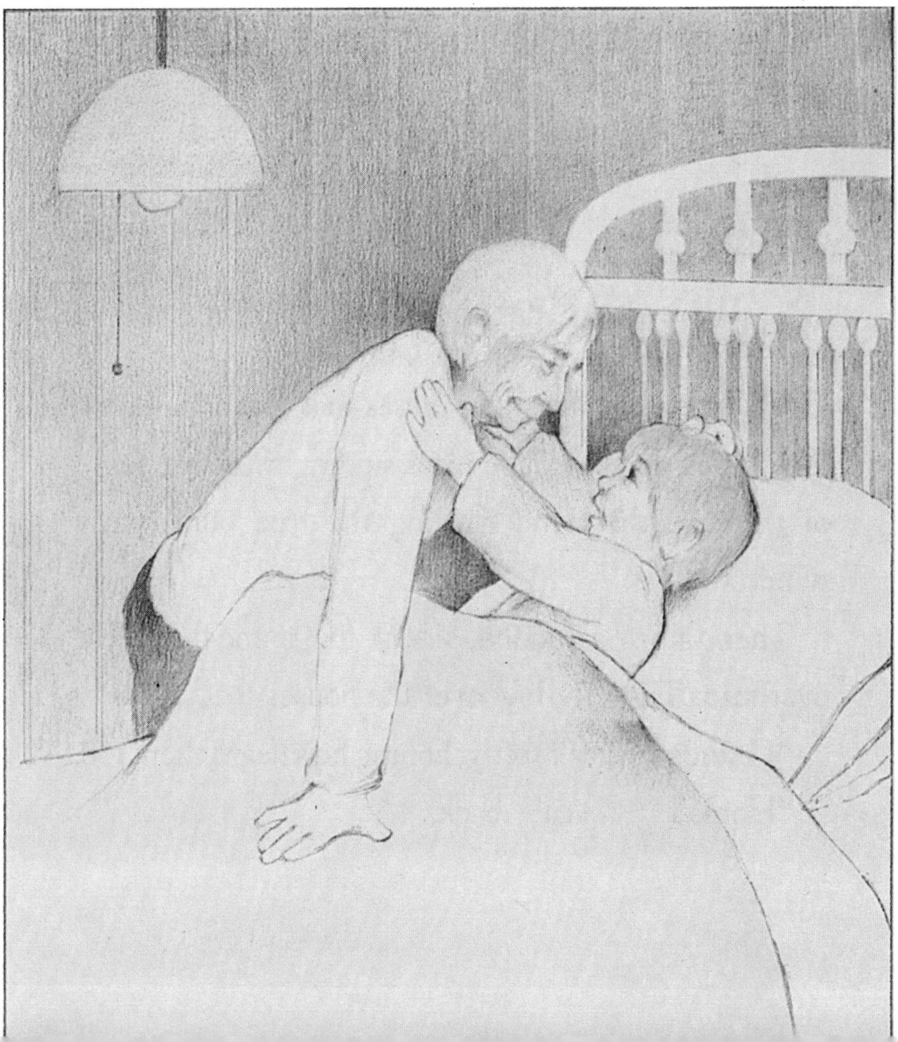

"Grandpa," I call, hoping he had heard them, too.

"Honkers," he calls back.

"They are honkers," I say to myself. I know. Because I'm looking through Grandpa's eyes.

Think About It

1. In what special ways did John "see" through Grandpa's eyes?
2. How did John use his fingers like a waterfall?
3. Why did Grandpa call the geese "honkers"?
4. How did John learn step by step the way that Grandpa "sees"?
5. On your desk, put some things in the order of a clock face. Close your eyes, and see if you can find what you want.

For a Quick Exit

by NORMA FARBER

For going up or coming down,
in big department stores in town,
you take an escalator.
(They come in pairs.)
Or else an elevator.
(Also stairs.)

I wish storekeepers would provide

a slide!

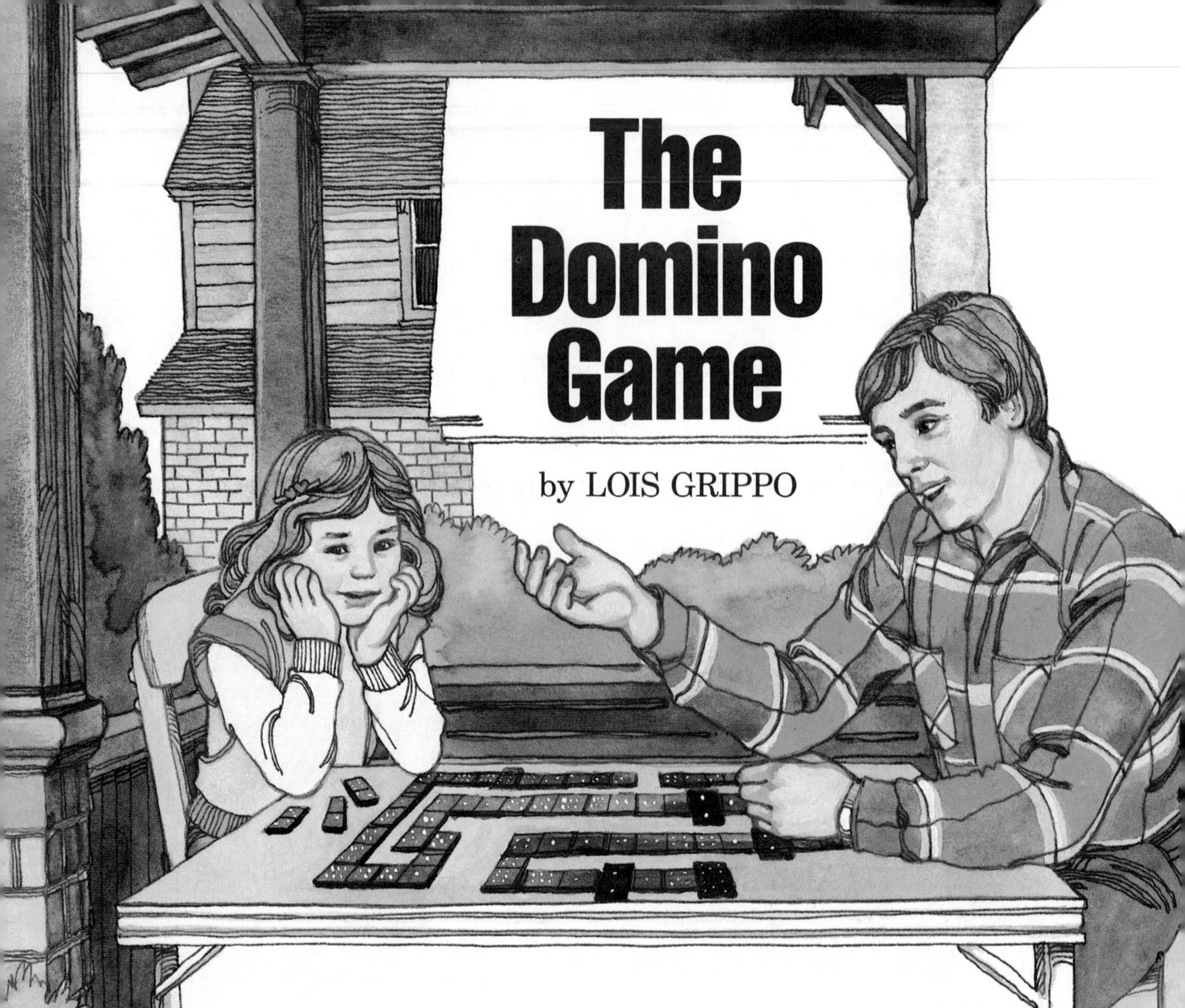

The Domino Game

by LOIS GRIPPO

On warm summer afternoons, my father and I often sit on the front porch and play dominoes. Most of the time, my father wins. When I grumble, he cheers me up by telling me of a time when he didn't always win at dominoes.

My father's friends call him *Edward*. But when he was my age, his friends all called him *Ed*. At that time, he didn't always win at games. He used to play dominoes with a girl named Wendy. Dad says Wendy was a lot like me.

Wendy was very good at all games, but her favorite game was dominoes.

One afternoon, Wendy won seven games in a row. My father began to grumble that he could never win, and he wouldn't play anymore. He got up and started to go straight home.

Wendy called after him. "Ed," she said, "we don't have to play this game. Let me show you a new and special way to use dominoes."

Wendy ran into her house and came back out carrying a big box. The box was almost as big as Wendy. It had something in it and looked as if it might just break right open.

"Come on, Ed," she cried excitedly. "I know a great new game that we can play."

But my father didn't feel like playing anything by then.

"I'm going home," he told Wendy.

Wendy watched Ed walk away. She shook her head and laughed. Then she opened the box. It was filled with loose dominoes. There were so many that it would have taken hours to count them all.

"I'll make a domino path," Wendy thought. "I'll use all of my dominoes to write a special message for Ed."

She began to set the dominoes one next to another. Wendy had planned what the message was going to be. She placed the dominoes in a wavy line all over the driveway next to her house.

Then Wendy asked Mr. Benson next door if she could put dominoes on his driveway.

Mr. Benson said "all right" and stood on his front porch watching Wendy build her path.

Wendy worked fast to put the dominoes in place. She smiled because of her secret plan. Finally, the dominoes were all placed exactly as she wanted them to be. Stretched across the two driveways, they looked like little black buildings with little white windows.

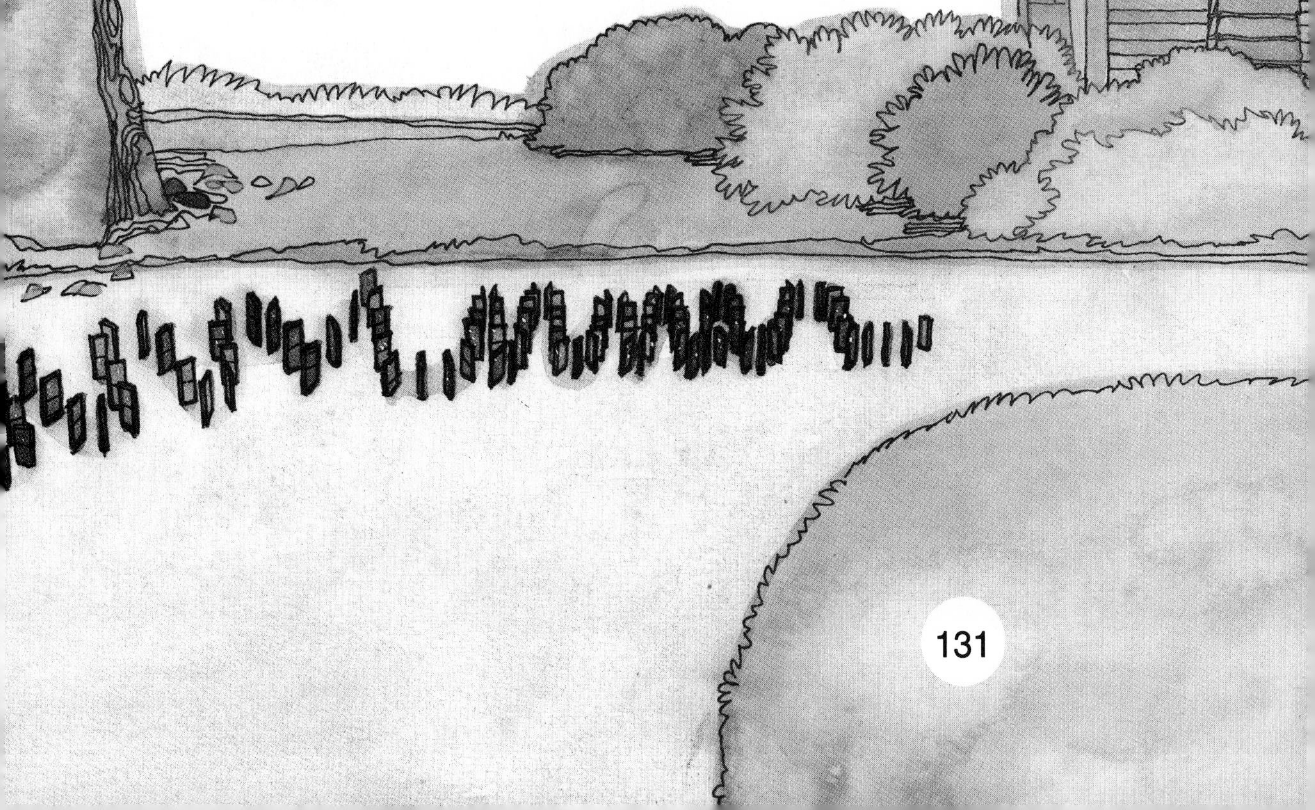

Dad says he heard Wendy call him. He decided to go and see what she was up to.

Wendy was so excited about her big surprise that she was hopping up and down. She quickly ran around the domino path to get back to the first domino.

Wendy laughed out loud. "Soon you'll see your special message, Ed," she said.

Mr. and Mrs. Cook, who lived next to Mr. Benson, heard the laughing. They came out and stood on their front steps to see what was happening.

Everyone looked very surprised at the long, zigzagging domino path. Wendy was very excited. Her big blue eyes danced as she shouted to all the people, "Watch, and you will see the surprise message that I made for Ed!"

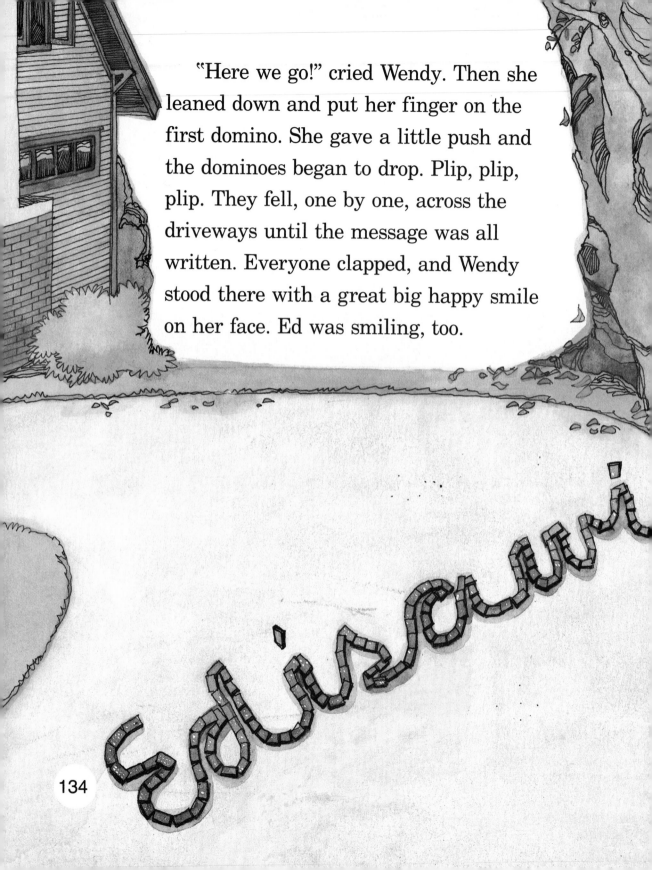

"Here we go!" cried Wendy. Then she leaned down and put her finger on the first domino. She gave a little push and the dominoes began to drop. Plip, plip, plip. They fell, one by one, across the driveways until the message was all written. Everyone clapped, and Wendy stood there with a great big happy smile on her face. Ed was smiling, too.

I love to hear my father tell the story of Wendy and the domino path. Maybe that's because I know a woman named Wendy. I call her *Mom*. She calls my father *Ed* and still thinks he is a winner.

READ ON!

Nu Dang and His Kite by Jacqueline Ayer. Nu Dang loved to fly his kite. One day, it floated away. Read about Nu Dang's travels to find his kite.

The Very Hungry Caterpillar by Eric Carle. Where do butterflies come from? Read this story to find out.

All Because I'm Older by Phyllis Naylor. John says that his little brother makes him do things he doesn't want to do. See if this is true.

A Nest of Wood Ducks by Evelyn Shaw. Read all about how one kind of bird raises its young.

The Summer Night by Charlotte Zolotow. Read what happens one summer night when a girl can't sleep.

UNIT 4

Waterways

LEARN NEW WORDS

1. The ice **disappeared** in the warm sun.
2. Sara asked me to do a **favor** for her.
3. When it is cool out, I put on a **jacket**.
4. I'm **jealous** because you have a new coat.
5. She pulled a cat from her **magical** hat.
6. He had more strength than he **realized**.
7. My jacket was **ruined** by the rain.
8. We looked at the **shimmering** lake.
9. I keep my **silver** ring in a small box.
10. The bird cried a **ghostly** cry.
11. The **island** is in the middle of the lake.
12. The ring was as **precious** as gold.

GET SET TO READ

What would it be like if the sun did not rise every morning?

Read the story to find out how the animals get the sun to rise.

The Silver Bay

adapted from a story
by FRANKLYN VARELA-PÉREZ

Long ago, Sea Gull lived on the small green island of Puerto Rico. Sea Gull was a magical bird dressed in a shimmering coat of silver feathers.

Every morning, before the sun rose, Sea Gull would look over the small bay. Gliding on a sea breeze, he would watch the white sand and splashing blue water. Then suddenly, he would magically race across the dark morning sky like a shimmering band of silver. That was the sign for all the night animals to go home and sleep.

One day when the sun was already up, Crab did not go home to sleep. He was jealous of Sea Gull's silver coat and planned to take it for himself.

"Hello, Sea Gull," jealous Crab called out. "I want to ask a favor. May I borrow your beautiful coat?"

"My coat?" cried Sea Gull, afraid. "If I give away my coat, the sun won't rise."

"Don't worry," said Crab, smiling. "The favor is only for today. I am going to visit Tree Lizard. He'll be so pleased to see the silver, shimmering coat."

Sea Gull felt that he couldn't refuse to do the favor. Tree Lizard was a good friend, and friends should be made happy.

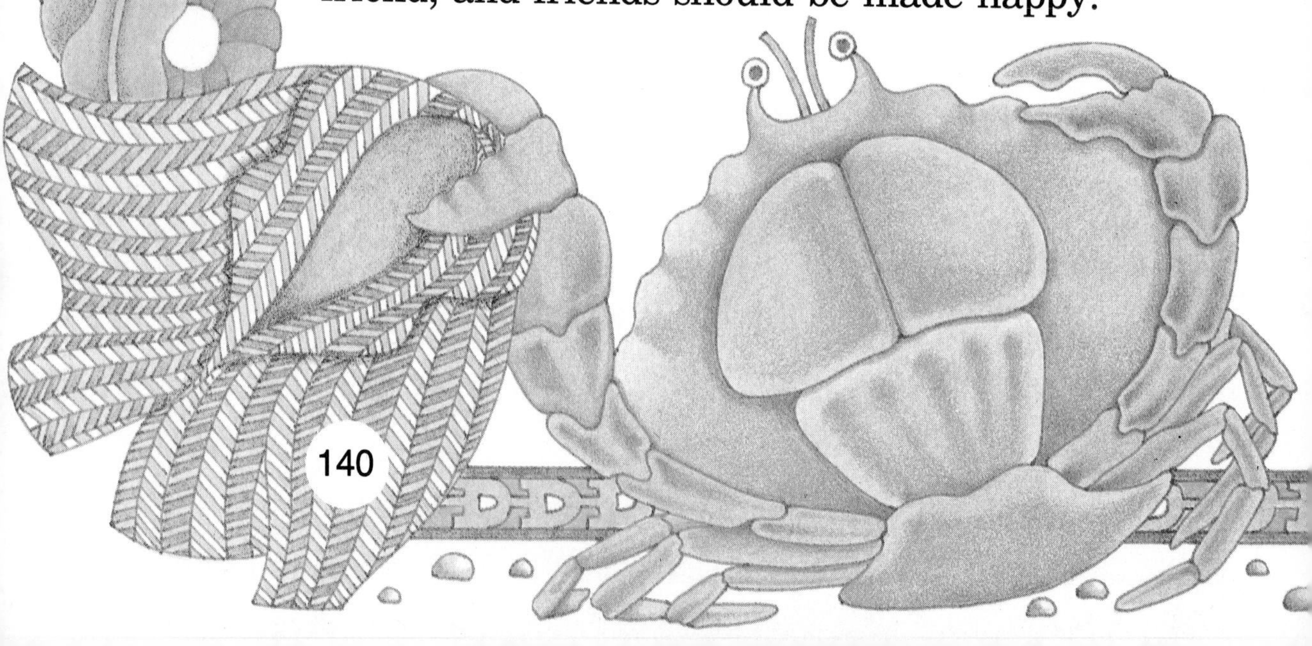

"All right," said Sea Gull. "You may borrow the silver coat. But what can I put on instead?"

"This," said Crab. In his claw was a dusty jacket of gray and white. "This jacket isn't as precious as your coat. But think how happy Tree Lizard will be."

So Sea Gull put on the dusty gray-and-white jacket. Crab disappeared into the jungle with the precious silver coat.

Soon, morning turned into afternoon. Afternoon turned into sunset, and sunset turned into the warm night. The night stretched out endlessly until it was one, two, three days long.

At last, Tree Lizard went looking for Sea Gull. "Sea Gull," called Tree Lizard, "why don't you wake the sun?"

Sea Gull answered, "I let Crab borrow my silver coat to visit you."

"That jealous crab never came to see me! I think he lied," said Tree Lizard.

Sea Gull flew out of his nest and soared in the sky. Then he saw Crab.

Crab was singing and dancing in the silver coat. When he saw Sea Gull coming, he tried to hide. He found a hole, but it wasn't big enough. Sea Gull was almost there, so Crab threw himself into the water with a splash.

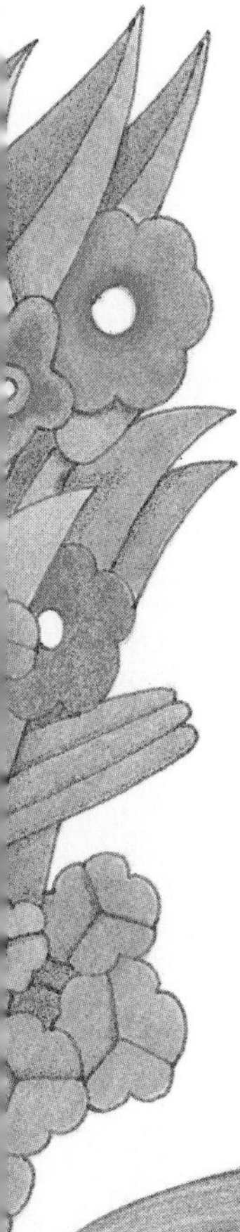

Then something awful happened. The beautiful coat started to lose its silver. The shimmering color left the coat and flowed over the splashing waves.

Sea Gull stared at the water and cried, "Now how will I ever wake the sun? The world will be dark forever."

Sea Gull realized that he needed help. He flew to Rooster's farm and called out, "Rooster, we are ruined! I have lost my precious silver coat and can't wake the sun. Help me!"

Rooster said, "Of course I'll help." Then he hopped to the top of the fence and crowed as loudly as he could.

The sound shook the sun out of sleep. "Where is Sea Gull?" asked the sun.

"He's lost his magical silver coat and couldn't awaken you," said Rooster.

The sun groaned a little and started the long climb up the horizon.

While the sun was rising, Crab splashed out of the water. He was sorry, but it was too late. The magical coat was ruined. Crab dropped it on the sand and disappeared into the jungle.

Sea Gull found his ruined coat. He realized that he would never again race like a silver band across the sky to wake the sun. He stood by the bay in his gray-and-white jacket and cried a ghostly cry.

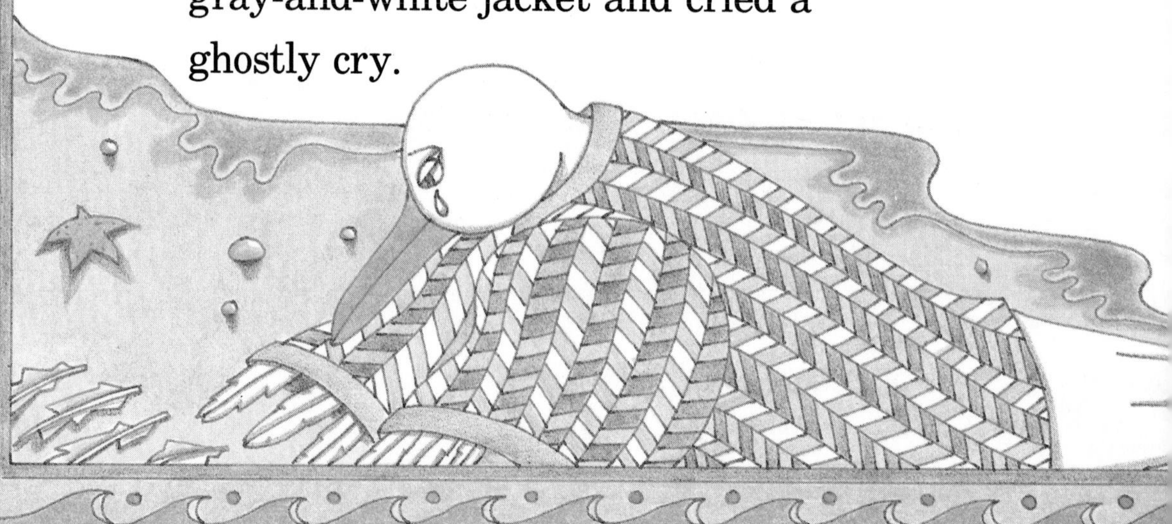

But not all of Sea Gull's magic was lost. You can still see it today in La Parguera, a bay on Puerto Rico's coast.

When the moon is full, the water shimmers like precious silver. You may even hear the ghostly cry of a sea gull.

Think About It

1. Why do you think Crab wanted Sea Gull's coat?
2. How did Sea Gull lose his coat?
3. What made the water turn silver?
4. What made the sun rise after Sea Gull lost his silver coat?
5. What things happen in this story that could not really happen?

LEARN NEW WORDS

1. My exercise class **begins** tomorrow.
2. I heard an old **familiar** tune today.
3. She reads for a **few** hours every day.
4. The **fisherman** worked on his boat.
5. Did you remember, or did you **forget**?
6. They **journeyed** to an island to rest.
7. You **reminded** me of a familiar old story.
8. I'm going swimming at the **seashore**.
9. No one spoke, so the room was **silent**.
10. The **turtles** poked out their heads.
11. The water gently **washed** over our toes.
12. The **wounded** fox lost its strength.
13. He planted beans in the rich **earth**.
14. The waves in the **ocean** were high today.

GET SET TO READ

What would it be like to live underwater? Read to see what happens when Urashima goes to a magic place underwater.

Seashore Story

adapted from a story
by TARO YASHIMA

Far away on an island at the southern tip of Japan is a seashore where city noises never come. The quiet of ancient times is there, as it always has been.

One day, a few school children and their teacher journeyed to this southern island to camp and sail. A fisherman on the shore and a few turtles on the silent beach reminded the children of an old and familiar story. It is the story of Urashima, the fisherman.

Urashima was an ancient fisherman who once saved the life of a wounded turtle. And so the story begins.

One day while Urashima was fishing, a turtle swam up to his boat. It was the same turtle that had been saved by the fisherman.

"Urashima! Urashima!" said the turtle. "You saved my life when I was wounded and about to die. Now I must do a favor for you. Get on my back, and I will take you to a beautiful place under the sea."

So Urashima climbed onto the turtle's back, and the turtle swam away, deep into the ocean. It was a long journey. Day after day and night after night, the deep waters washed over them.

At last, they reached a huge gate at the bottom of the sea. Beyond the gate, there rose a palace more grand than Urashima had ever dreamed.

Urashima and the turtle silently glided within the walls of the palace. There, placed before them, was a feast of food that tasted sweet, but strange.

Day followed day, and night followed night. The happy times went on, and no one counted the days or years. The sun no longer shone on Urashima's face. He forgot everything he had left behind.

But one day, Urashima thought about his fishing boat and his home. He was reminded of the sun, the warm earth, and his own people. He felt a great longing for them, and he decided to go back home. The sea people gave him a beautiful box as a good-by gift.

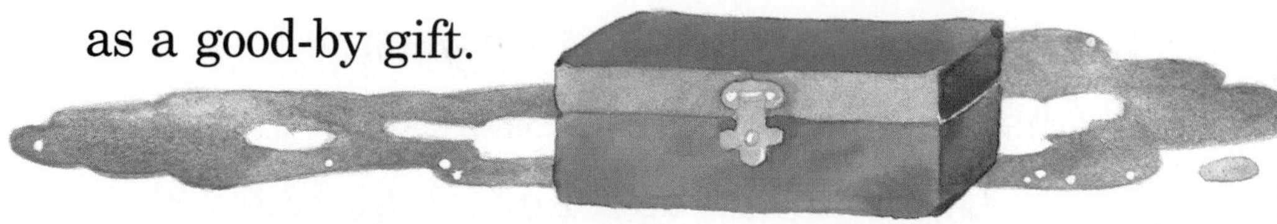

Once again, the turtle and Urashima made a long journey through the sea. When they reached the seashore where the earth was warm and where they had first met, the turtle said good-by to Urashima.

But when Urashima got to his town, there was not one face that he knew. Not one house was familiar.

Where was his own house? Gone! Where was his family? No one knew them. "There must be some mistake! How could everyone forget them?" Urashima wondered.

The mountain was the only place that looked the same to Urashima. He climbed the mountain to open his precious box.

He opened the box, and only a thin line of white smoke rose from the box and flowed in the air around Urashima. At once, he turned into a very old man.

That was the end of the tale of Urashima, the fisherman. A few children on the beach began to talk about it.

"Was there really a palace at the bottom of the ocean?" asked one.

"Well, that was what the ancient people believed," said another.

Suddenly, a girl who had been silent spoke up. "But why had his house disappeared?" she asked. "And why had his family gone? And why did only smoke flow out of the beautiful box?"

"Because he stayed away too long," said the teacher. "You must always come back on time. It would not have happened if he did not forget the people he loved."

The children thought for a while, saying not a word. Some of them were beginning to understand what the teacher had said. Only the youngest ones were not satisfied. "Even so," they said, "something better should have come out of the box."

"Yes, something much better . . . "

An ocean breeze was blowing the children's voices into the sky. Even the birds in the sky seemed to be listening. The sun went down, and the soft noise of the waves washed against the shore. It was the end of the day.

Think About It

1. What happened when Urashima went under the ocean?
2. What changes did Urashima see when he came home?
3. What did the children learn from the story of Urashima?
4. What magic things are in this story and in the story about Sea Gull?
5. Tell how the story might have ended if something better had been in the box.

On Our Bikes

by LILLIAN MORRISON

The roads to the beach
                    are winding
  we glide down
            breeze-whipped
curving
               past hills of sand
   pedal and coast
      through wide smell of the sea
         old familiar sunfeel
    windwallop.
Race you to the water's edge!

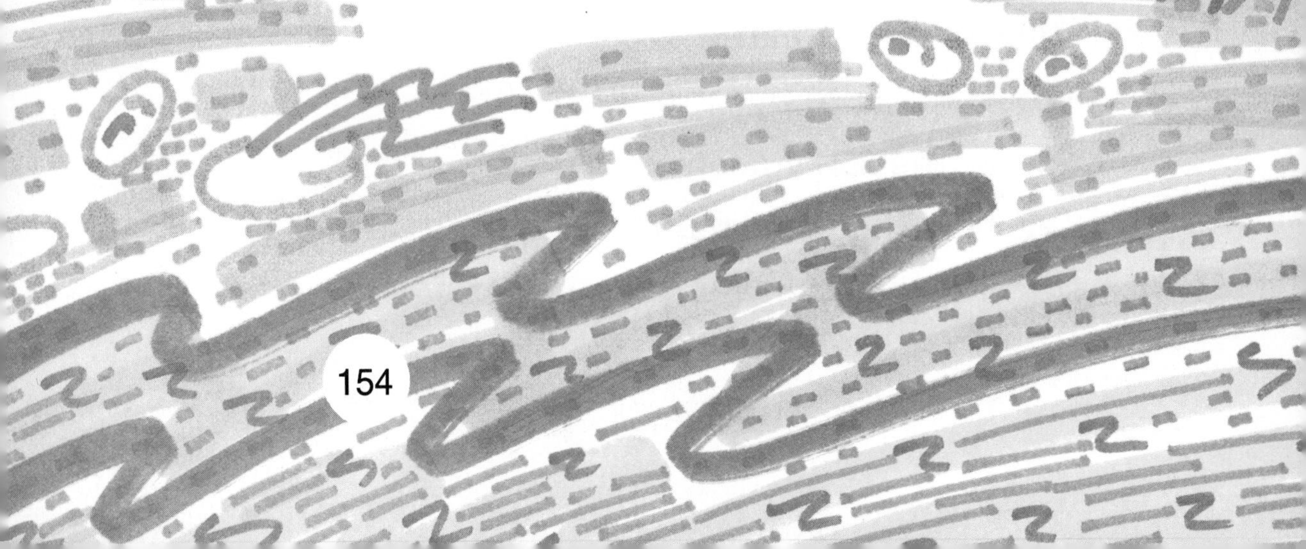

Make-Believe and Real

In "Seashore Story," Urashima did some things that real people could not do. He also did some things that real people *could* do. Some of the things he did were make-believe, and some were not. Could real people go fishing? Could real people live under the sea? Why or why not?

Some of the stories you read are make-believe, but they have parts that could be real. Which of these sentences could be facts?

1. Sixty huge purple flowers screeched noisily at the ghostly sky.
2. The shy deer watched the geese fly silently overhead.

This is a make-believe story. Read it and think about the parts that are facts and the parts that are make-believe.

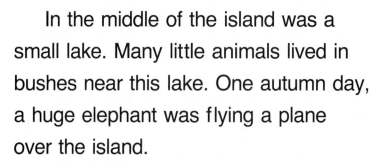

In the middle of the island was a small lake. Many little animals lived in bushes near this lake. One autumn day, a huge elephant was flying a plane over the island.

Suddenly, at sixty feet in the air, the plane stopped flying. The elephant pilot escaped by jumping out of the plane and splashing into the lake. After that, there was no more water in the lake. The animals needed water, so the elephant borrowed some from a well and filled up the lake.

Which parts of the story are facts? Which parts of it are make-believe?

LEARN NEW WORDS

1. We went to a **clearing** in the meadow.
2. Nikki **giggles** at all my jokes.
3. The twelve animals **huddle** together in the rain.
4. That girl is bright and **merry**.
5. The cat was **shivering** in the cold.
6. I swapped a **tiny** toy for a big toy.

GET SET TO READ

What would you do if you had to share something very small with many people?

As you read, see how something small was shared by many friends.

Mushroom in the Rain

adapted from a story
by MIRRA GINSBURG

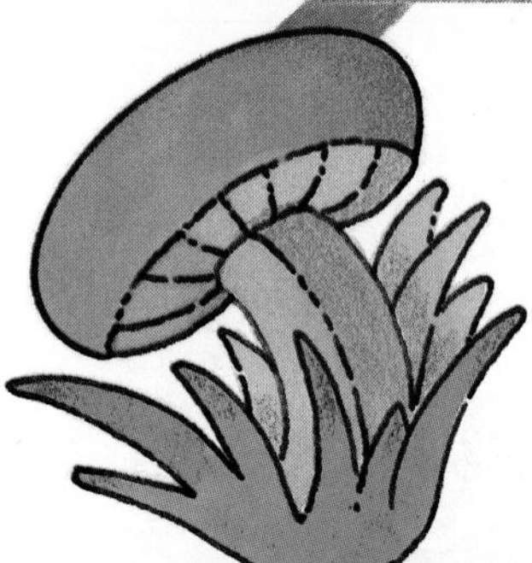

The Players:

MUSHROOM
ANT
BUTTERFLY
MOUSE
SPARROW
RABBIT
FOX
FROG

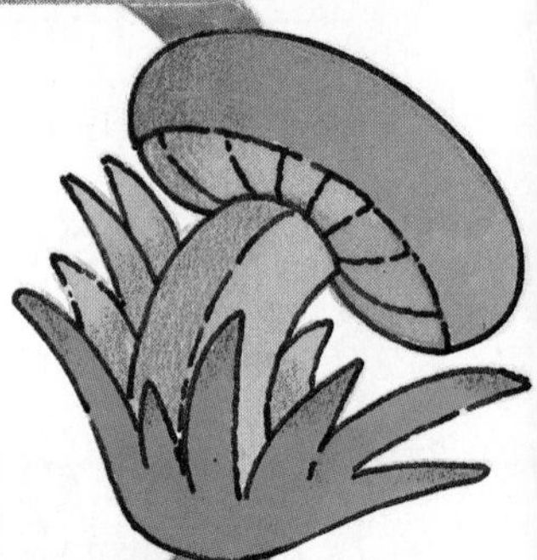

Time: Now

Place: A clearing in a meadow

(A mushroom sits alone in a clearing in a meadow.)

MUSHROOM: It was such a cheery, sunny day until now. Now the rain is coming down on me. It hasn't rained so hard for over a month. Oh my, I am getting wet!

(An ant comes looking for a place to hide from the rain. The ant is shivering and sneezing.)

Ant: Where can I go? Brr. Oh good, there is a mushroom. It's a tiny mushroom, but I think I can slip under it.

(The ant runs under the mushroom. A butterfly comes in, shaking her purple wings.)

Butterfly: Brother Ant, let me come in from the rain. I am so wet I cannot fly.

Ant: How can I let you in? There is barely room enough for one.

Butterfly: It doesn't matter. We can huddle together. It's better to be crowded than wet.

MUSHROOM: Move over, Ant, and make room for the butterfly. The rain is coming down harder and harder. Soon I will be standing in a big puddle!

(A mouse comes running in, looking for a place to hide from the rain. She sees the mushroom and runs over to it.)

MOUSE: Please, do me a favor. Let me in under the mushroom. I am wet.

BUTTERFLY: We are wet ourselves! How can we let you in? There is no room.

MOUSE: But I am tiny. Just move a little closer. I am getting wetter and wetter!

MUSHROOM: Butterfly and Ant, huddle closer, and let the mouse in. The rain is coming down on me as if the clouds had burst. It just won't stop!

(A sparrow hops in.)

SPARROW *(Crying)*: My feathers are dripping. My wings are so tired that I can barely fly. My eyes are blinded by the heavy rain. Let me in under the mushroom until the rain stops!

MOUSE: But there is no more room here.

SPARROW: Please move over a tiny bit.

MUSHROOM: Can you make room for the sparrow?

(A rabbit arrives in the clearing.)

RABBIT: If I do not find a place to hide, that sly fox will surely catch me!

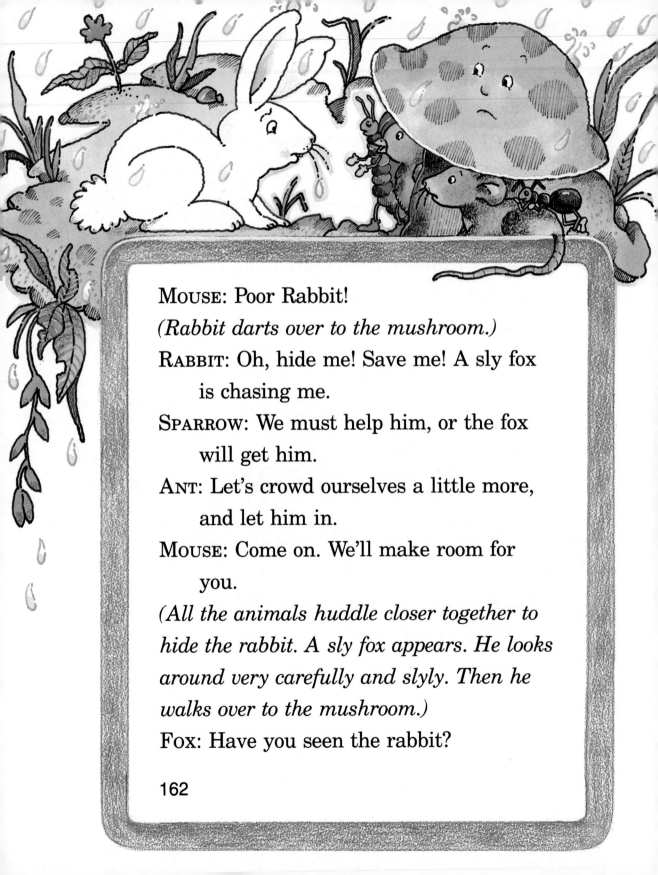

Mouse: Poor Rabbit!

(Rabbit darts over to the mushroom.)

Rabbit: Oh, hide me! Save me! A sly fox is chasing me.

Sparrow: We must help him, or the fox will get him.

Ant: Let's crowd ourselves a little more, and let him in.

Mouse: Come on. We'll make room for you.

(All the animals huddle closer together to hide the rabbit. A sly fox appears. He looks around very carefully and slyly. Then he walks over to the mushroom.)

Fox: Have you seen the rabbit?

BUTTERFLY: What rabbit? You must be mistaken!

FOX: I am not mistaken! Which way did he go?

MOUSE: Look! Do you see any sign of him? What makes you think a rabbit's in here?

(The sly fox begins sniffing around the mushroom.)

FOX *(Slyly)*: I'll just bet he's in there!

BUTTERFLY: You silly fox! How could a rabbit be in here? We barely have enough room for ourselves.

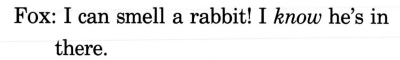

FOX: I can smell a rabbit! I *know* he's in there.

SPARROW: Don't you see there isn't a single bit of room? Try the next mushroom!

FOX: I'll find that rabbit. I will!

(The fox turns up his nose, flicks his tail, and runs off. Everyone giggles.)

ALL THE ANIMALS: Hurrah! Hurrah!

Mushroom: The rain is over! Here comes the sun from behind the clouds. Everyone, come out into the sun where it's bright and merry.

(A line of animals comes out from under the mushroom.)

Sparrow: Hurrah! The sun is out!

Mouse: The sun feels nice and warm.

Rabbit: What a beautiful day it turned out to be! I thought the rain would go on and on.

(Frog hops into the clearing.)

Ant: There is one thing I don't understand. At first, there was barely room under the tiny mushroom. In the end, all five of us were able to sit under it!

Frog: Ribba-ha-ha, ribba-ha-ha.

Butterfly: Why are you so merry, Frog? What makes you giggle so? What is the matter with you?

FROG: Ribba-ha-ha. Don't you know what happens to a mushroom in the rain? Ribba-ha-ha.

(The frog hops away, giggling.)

MOUSE: What happens to a mushroom in the rain?

BUTTERFLY: I don't know.

SPARROW: Do you know, Rabbit?

RABBIT: No, I don't. Do you know, Ant?

ANT: Not me.

MUSHROOM: Well, take a good look at me.

(The animals stand back and look hard at Mushroom.)

Mushroom: Now *you* are giggling. Suddenly you know why there was room for every single one of you. Tell me, what happens to a mushroom when it rains?

All the Animals *(Bursting out laughing)*: IT GROWS!!!!!

Think About It

1. How could the small space under Mushroom be shared by many friends?
2. How did the animals under Mushroom show they were brave and kind?
3. Tell how the animals might have stayed dry if they had not seen Mushroom.
4. How is the thing you use to keep dry on a rainy day like a mushroom?
5. Draw a picture of things you can use on a rainy day.

The Lake That Disappeared

by CHRISTINE ECONOMOS

"Hi, Mom! I'm home," called Alison as she burst through the door. She shook the water off her raincoat and thought, "What an awful day! I just can't wait for summer to come."

Alison was shivering in her rainy-day clothes when she heard her mother call.

"A letter came for you from the camp that you're going to this summer."

"I wonder what it says," Alison said as she stopped shivering. "Where is the letter?"

"It's on the living-room table," said her mother.

Alison found the letter on the table and opened it. This is what it said:

Dear Alison,

We all know how excited you are about coming to Bushy Hill Camp this summer. We are writing to all campers to let them know about something that happened. OUR LAKE DISAPPEARED! A big dam nearby burst, and there is no water left to fill the lake. The lake has dried up.

Please don't be too unhappy. We have worked out many ways to enjoy ourselves. I'm sure we'll all have a wonderful summer.

Margo Schwab, Camp Director

"Mom!" yelled Alison. "The lake disappeared. This can't happen. My first summer at camp and the lake disappears!"

"Alison, what's the matter?" asked her mother as she ran into the living room.

"Mom, the letter from the camp says the lake disappeared," cried Alison. "Camp will be ruined without a lake. We won't be able to have any fun in the water at all!"

"What? That can't be!" said her mother. "Let me see the letter."

Alison handed the letter to her mother.

"I don't understand this," said her mother. "How can a lake disappear? Call Cathy. This will be her third year at the camp. Maybe she will know something."

Alison called Cathy. "Hello, Cathy? I just got a letter from the camp."

"I did, too," said Cathy. "The lake has dried up. Maybe we can swim in the Bushy Hill Duck Pond."

"But how could the lake disappear?" asked Alison.

"I don't know," said Cathy. "It has something to do with the dam. Don't worry. Maybe it will rain hard, and the lake will fill up before we get there."

At dinner that night, Alison hardly spoke. She couldn't hide the unhappiness that showed on her face. She couldn't hold back the tears.

"It will be all right," said her father.

"Cathy said the lake was the best part of all," said Alison.

"You'll still have a good time," said her mother. "Wait and see. Sometimes, a thing that makes us unhappy at first has a very happy ending."

The day finally arrived for Alison to leave for camp. Once her camp clothes and blankets were put into the car, Alison and her family began the long journey to Bushy Hill Camp.

"We'll find out what happened to the lake when we get there," said Alison's father.

"Maybe Cathy was right, and rain filled the lake," said Alison, full of hope.

At last, they arrived at camp. Alison stared through the car window. "Look at that huge hole!" she cried.

"That must be where the lake was," said her mother. "It looks pretty awful."

The camp was a busy place. Campers were carrying bundles to little log houses. They were saying good-by to their parents and hello to last summer's friends.

When everyone had put their things away and all the parents had gone home, the camp leader called the campers together. "As you know, we won't be able to use the lake this year," she said. "But we'll have a great summer anyway."

Just then, a man walked into the camp. He waved to the camp leader. Then he went over and spoke to her for a few seconds. The campers huddled near the two of them, trying to hear.

The camp director nodded to the man and smiled. Then she turned to the girls and said, "I have some very good news. First, I would like you to meet our neighbor, Mr. Messer. Mr. Messer owns the big lake near the camp. He has offered to let us borrow it for the summer. Let's give him a big cheer."

The girls burst out cheering!

The next week was a busy one. The girls went swimming under the warm summer sky. Sometimes, they took boat rides across the lake. They named it *Lake Messer*.

Mr. Messer came by now and then. He would tell the girls about the fish in the lake or about the unusual trees nearby. He was happy to see everyone having a good time on his lake.

One day, Alison wrote her family this letter.

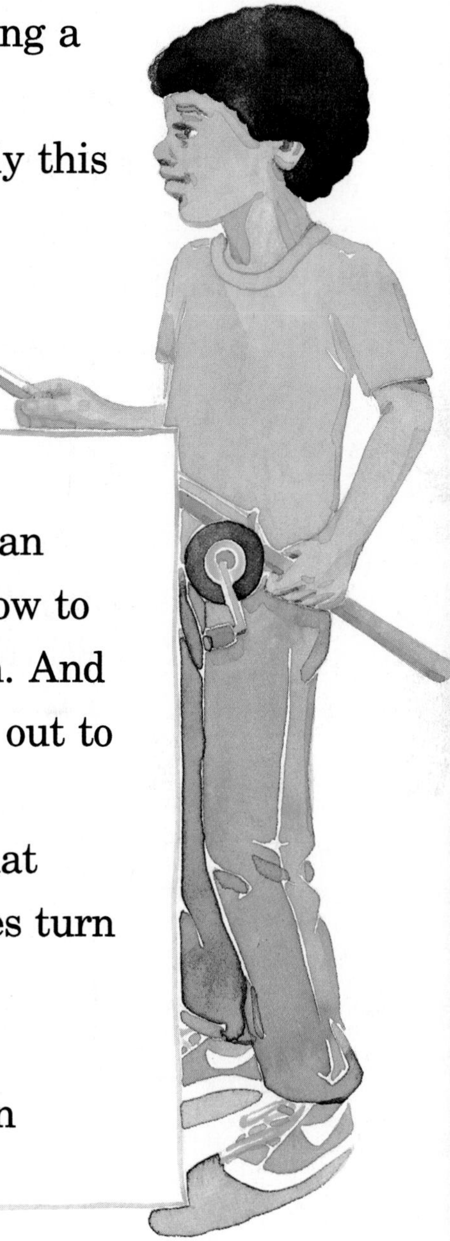

Dear Mom and Dad,

We got a lake! It belongs to a man called Mr. Messer. He showed us how to imitate bird sounds and how to fish. And do you know what? My fish turned out to be an old slipper!

You were right, Mom! Things that make us unhappy at first sometimes turn out to have happy endings.

Love,
Alison

READ ON!

The Maggie B. by Irene Haas. Margaret sails away on *The Maggie B.* Read about the exciting times she has.

The Foggy Rescue by Consuelo Joerns. The Mouse family gets lost at sea. Read to find out what happens.

Three by the Sea by Edward Marshall. Lolly and her friends tell stories to pass the time. See which story you like best.

Pea Soup and Sea Serpents by William Schroder. Read this story to find out what happens when two young boys go out in a boat.

Rain Rain Rivers by Uri Shulevitz. Read to find out all the things a young girl learns about rain.

UNIT 5

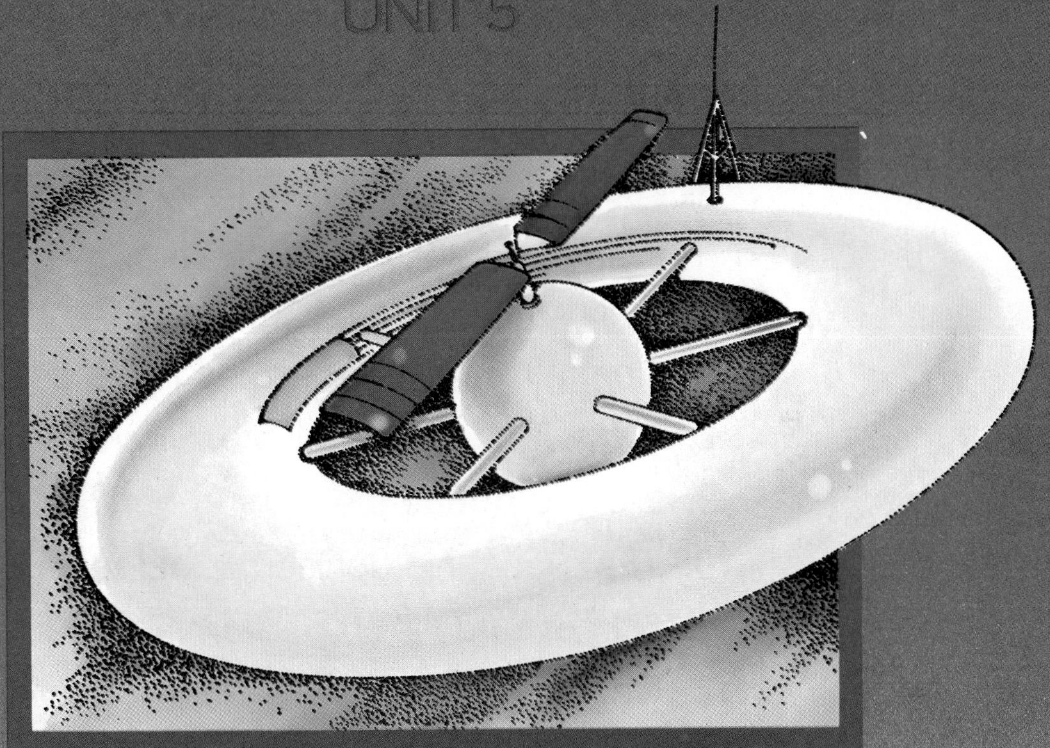

Imagination Station

LEARN NEW WORDS

1. Do **alligators** belong in hot, wet places?
2. I found a **cork** in this old water jar.
3. The sunset this **evening** was beautiful.
4. He stretched out in the **hammock**.
5. We cut a path through the **jungle**.
6. To build a doghouse, we need **lumber**.
7. He put his bag of **marbles** in the box.
8. My **neighbors** are all friendly people.
9. Did you **notice** the color of her kite?
10. The sly cat hid behind the **palm** tree.
11. I'm not sure which **person** laughed.
12. On top of the house was a tall **tower**.

GET SET TO READ

What might you do if the color of your room changed overnight?

Read to find out what Mr. Plumbean does when a funny thing happens to his house.

The Big Orange Splot

adapted from a story
by DANIEL MANUS PINKWATER

Mr. Plumbean lived on a street where all the houses were the same. He liked it that way, and so did everyone else on Mr. Plumbean's street. "This is a neat street," they would all say.

Then one day, a sea gull flew over Mr. Plumbean's house. The sea gull was carrying a can of orange paint. (No one knew why.) It made a big orange splot on Mr. Plumbean's house.

"Too bad!" all of the neighbors said. "Now Mr. Plumbean will have to paint his house again."

"I suppose I will," said Mr. Plumbean. But he didn't paint his house right away. Instead, he stood and looked at the orange splot on his house. He looked for a long, long time.

After a while, the neighbors grew tired of seeing that big orange splot. Someone said, "Mr. Plumbean, we wish you'd get around to painting your house."

"Okay," said Mr. Plumbean.

He took some blue paint and some white paint, and that night he got busy. He painted at night because it was cooler. When the blue paint and the white paint were gone, he got red paint, yellow paint, green paint, and purple paint.

In the morning, Mr. Plumbean's house was like a rainbow. It was also like a jungle.

There was the big orange splot, and there were little orange splots. There were stripes. There were pictures of elephants, alligators, and rocket ships.

The neighbors looked at the rainbow of colors and said, "Plumbean has popped his cork, flipped his wig, and blown his stack." They went away, talking angrily.

That day, Mr. Plumbean bought lumber and tools. That night, he built a tower on top of his roof, and he painted a clock on the tower.

The next day, the neighbors said, "Plumbean has popped his cork, lost his marbles, and doesn't know which end is up." Then they decided they would pretend not to notice.

That night, Mr. Plumbean got a truck filled with green things. He planted palm trees, baobabs, and other jungle trees. In the morning, he bought a hammock and a real alligator.

When the other people came out of their houses, they saw Mr. Plumbean lying in a hammock between two palm trees. They noticed the alligator lying in the grass, too. Mr. Plumbean was having an orange drink.

"Plumbean has gone too far!"

"This used to be a neat street!"

"Plumbean, what have you done to your house?" the people shouted.

"My house is me, and I am it. My house is where I like to be, and it looks like all my dreams," Mr. Plumbean said.

The people went away. But first, they asked the person who lived next door to Mr. Plumbean to go and have a talk with him. "Tell him we all liked it here before he changed his house. Tell him that his house has to be the same as ours so that we can have a neat street."

The man went to see Mr. Plumbean that evening. They sat under the palm trees having an orange drink and talking all evening long.

Early the next morning, the man went out to buy lumber, pieces of rope, nails, and paint. When the people came out of their houses, they saw a red-and-yellow ship next door to the house of Mr. Plumbean.

"What have you done to your house?" the neighbors shouted at the man.

"My house is me, and I am it. My house is where I like to be. Now it looks like all my dreams," said the man, who had always loved ships.

"You're just like Plumbean," the people said. "You've lost your marbles, and you have bats in your belfry."

Then, one by one, the neighbors went to see Mr. Plumbean in the evening. They would sit under the palm trees and have an orange drink and talk about their dreams. Whenever anyone visited Mr. Plumbean's house, the very next day that person would set about changing his or her house. Soon, all the houses fit the dreams of their owners.

Whenever a stranger came to the street of Mr. Plumbean and his neighbors, the stranger would say, "This is not a neat street."

Then all the people would answer, "Our street is where we like to be, and it looks like all our dreams."

Think About It

1. What does Mr. Plumbean do when a funny thing happens to his house?
2. How did the neighbors feel about the changes that Mr. Plumbean made?
3. What happened after the neighbors went to talk to Mr. Plumbean?
4. How did Mr. Plumbean and his neighbors use their dreams to change their houses?
5. Draw a picture of *your* dream house.

LEARN NEW WORDS

1. The hills were far **below** the clouds.
2. I want to go, and **besides**, Dad is going.
3. She **collected** pictures of animals.
4. The **dragons** are big and make fire.
5. Which animals have only one **horn**?
6. Name some **make-believe** animals.
7. On **Monday** we went to the fair.
8. She was awake when I **returned**.
9. Put this **saddle** on the spotted horse.
10. Will you **wear** your new coat to school?
11. Each of the **unicorns** had a horn on its head.
12. Two days after Monday is **Wednesday**.

GET SET TO READ

Imagine that you were able to fly away to exciting places.

Read to find out how Carmen goes on a magic journey.

Unicorn Days

by JUDITH ROSENBAUM

Chapter One

The first time Carmen ever heard of unicorns was the one Monday her friend Juan showed her his book about make-believe animals. The book had many dragons. On one page, there was a picture of an animal that Carmen had never seen before.

It looked like a white horse with pale gold hooves. But on the unicorn's head was a single, twisting horn. It gleamed like silvery glass. Below the picture was the word *unicorn*.

From that moment on, the unicorn was Carmen's favorite make-believe animal. She read everything she could find. She collected pictures. She put up one big picture against her wall. She started collecting and swapping unicorn stickers. She would wear a sticker on her jacket.

One Wednesday afternoon, Carmen said to Juan, "I wish unicorns were real."

"Unicorns are *not* real," said Juan. "Besides, I like dragons better myself."

But Carmen did not give up wishing. Maybe there were *some* real unicorns. "I still wish I could meet one," she said. "A unicorn would make a great friend."

On the way to school the next morning, Carmen noticed something ghostly pale flash by. But when she turned to look, there was nothing.

That afternoon, Carmen ran into her yard to play, and there she saw it—a unicorn! Her eyes hadn't lied to her.

The unicorn was even more wonderful than its pictures. Its coat was as white as the new moon. Its hooves were pale gold. Its single, twisting horn gleamed.

"What are you doing here?" whispered Carmen, staring at the animal.

"You wished for me, and I appeared," said the unicorn.

Carmen stared harder.

The unicorn went on, "Besides, I was wishing for a friend, too. Climb on my back, and we'll fly to faraway places."

"Yes, yes!" said Carmen as she jumped on the unicorn's back. The unicorn wasn't wearing a saddle, but Carmen found that she didn't need one. A unicorn is easy to ride without a saddle. Then the unicorn jumped straight up into the air, and it flew. Things were really getting more exciting!

Carmen looked down at the busy streets below her, but nobody looked up. "No one can see us," said the unicorn. "When we are together, people can only see us when I let them. Now, where do you want to go? I can fly you anywhere and still have you home each evening in time for dinner."

"Anywhere?" asked Carmen. "Then I want to see China."

"China, here we come!" said the unicorn.

Carmen and the unicorn soared up high, right under the clouds. They flew to the other side of the world, where it was night. They flew past midnight and into morning. Then Carmen looked down and saw China lying far below. She saw its mountains and wide rivers. China was a big land, but it looked small from high up in the sky. She saw the Great Wall snaking across the land.

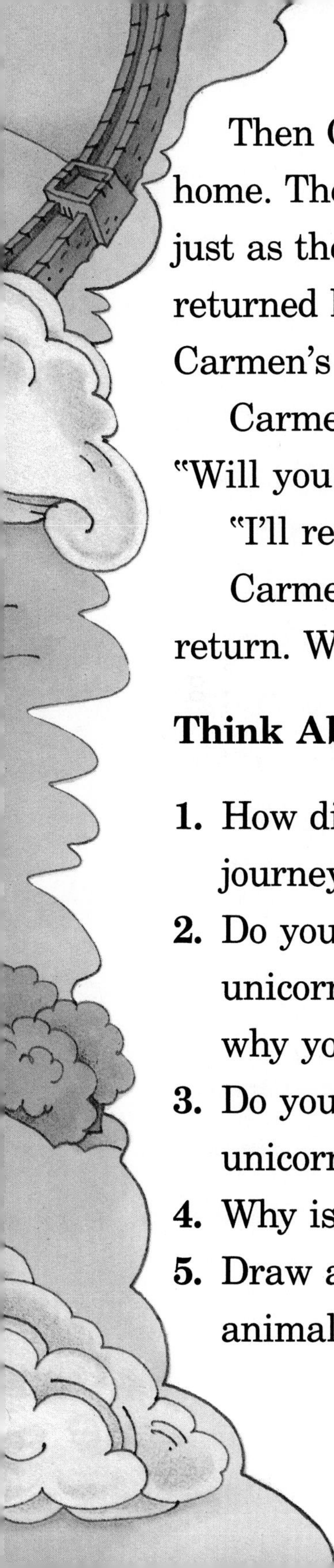

Then Carmen and the unicorn flew home. They seemed to fly for hours. But just as the unicorn had promised, they returned home that evening in time for Carmen's dinner.

Carmen watched the unicorn fly away. "Will you come back?" she called.

"I'll return soon," it answered.

Carmen waited. But the unicorn didn't return. Would she ever see it again?

Think About It

1. How did Carmen go on a magic journey?
2. Do you think Carmen imagined the unicorn, or did it really appear? Tell why you think so.
3. Do you think Carmen will ever see the unicorn again? Why?
4. Why is it fun to imagine things?
5. Draw a picture of a make-believe animal. Tell what you think it can do.

LEARN NEW WORDS

1. When I moved here, I **became** his friend.
2. I'm **interested** in listening to music.
3. Tell me what you see in the **mirror**.
4. They headed straight **north**.
5. We shivered during the ice **storm**.
6. We saw lightning and heard **thunder**.
7. Let's **wander** around the fairgrounds.
8. Carmen wants to go on an **adventure**.
9. In which **direction** will they fly?
10. In an **emergency**, call a doctor.
11. You'll never **guess** where we're going.
12. He can see his **reflection** in the mirror.
13. The **statues** were made of clay.

GET SET TO READ

Sometimes, friends can help each other. Read to see how Carmen helps her new friend, the unicorn.

Unicorn Days

Chapter Two

Two weeks later, the unicorn returned at last. It said, "I'm sorry I couldn't come before, but there was an emergency up north. I helped a dragon put out a fire."

"That's all right," said Carmen. "I guess unicorns are kept pretty busy."

"We are," said the unicorn. "But today we can go on an adventure."

After that, Carmen and the unicorn enjoyed many adventures. They flew around the world in each direction. On a far desert island, they saw giant turtles racing on the beach. They even flew under the sea and heard whales singing.

Then one Wednesday, Carmen said, "Unicorn, I'm interested in learning about your home. What is it like?"

The unicorn looked at Carmen with unhappiness in its eyes. Its horn even seemed to gleam a little less, and it said, "Tragg the Terrible has turned my home into a land of ice. I was the only animal that got away. Now I can't return home, and I have to wander and wander from place to place. I was very lonely before you became my friend."

"How awful!" said Carmen. "But maybe I can help."

"Maybe you can," said Unicorn. "Tragg's magic can't hurt children."

Carmen said, "I will try. Please take me home so that I can get my emergency kit."

When she reached home, Carmen put on her warmest coat and hat. She took out her emergency kit. Inside her kit were helpful things such as extra string, paper, and pencils. There was a folding rain hat, some orange marbles, and a flashlight. Besides those things, there was a mirror that she used for mirror writing. With her kit, Carmen was ready for anything.

She climbed onto the unicorn's back, and the two of them flew off.

The unicorn flew north, then west, then north again. After a while, Carmen couldn't guess in what direction they were going. She thought they might be going in a southern direction. But maybe Unicorn's home was beyond the rainbow!

At last, Carmen saw land below. The unicorn glided to the ground. Carmen could see that snow and ice covered everything, even the trees. Even the animals were covered with ice and snow. They looked like marble statues.

Suddenly, Carmen saw a streak of lightning and heard thunder roll like an angry dragon. "Is a storm coming?" she asked.

"That's not a storm. That's Tragg!" cried the unicorn.

Lightning flashed, and thunder rolled again. A giant with angry eyes seemed to appear from nowhere. It was Tragg.

"So you are back, Unicorn!" he roared. Sparks flew from Tragg's hands. "You won't get away from me this time! I'll throw ice and snow at you, Unicorn. You will look like a statue, too."

Tragg stared down at Carmen, and sparks flashed from his angry eyes!

Carmen knew she had to do something right away. Quickly, she reached into her emergency kit. She saw her mirror and suddenly had an idea. "Maybe if the mirror catches Tragg's reflection, it will catch some of his magic," she thought.

Carmen held up the mirror to Tragg's awful face, and for a moment, Carmen, Tragg, and the unicorn stood still. Carmen and the unicorn held their breath! Suddenly, blue sparks flashed from the mirror, and lightning lit up the sky. Tragg saw his reflection in the mirror and froze into a huge block of ice! He became frozen by his own bad magic! Now he was a statue!

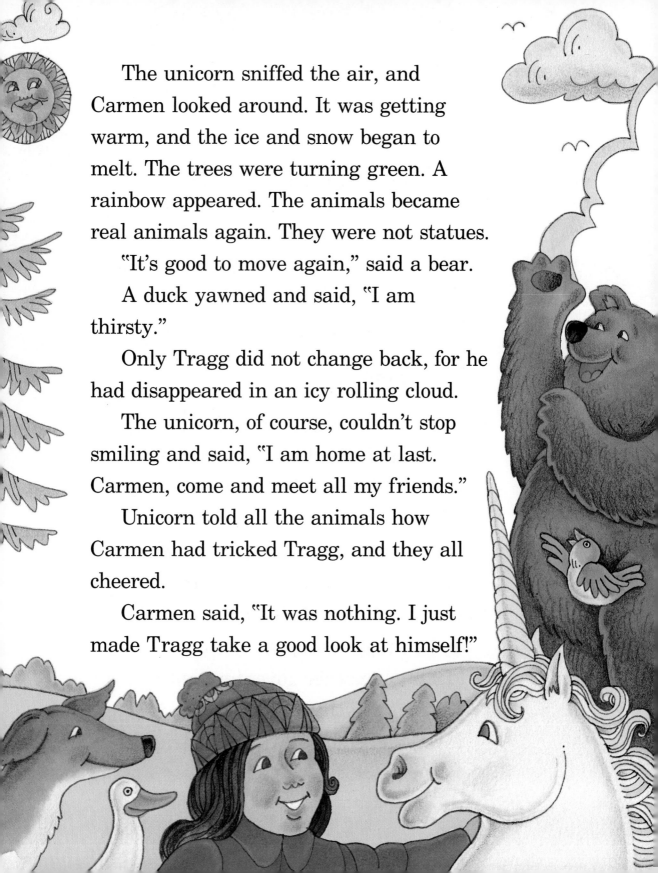

The unicorn sniffed the air, and Carmen looked around. It was getting warm, and the ice and snow began to melt. The trees were turning green. A rainbow appeared. The animals became real animals again. They were not statues.

"It's good to move again," said a bear.

A duck yawned and said, "I am thirsty."

Only Tragg did not change back, for he had disappeared in an icy rolling cloud.

The unicorn, of course, couldn't stop smiling and said, "I am home at last. Carmen, come and meet all my friends."

Unicorn told all the animals how Carmen had tricked Tragg, and they all cheered.

Carmen said, "It was nothing. I just made Tragg take a good look at himself!"

Then Carmen turned to the unicorn. She said sadly, "I'm glad you have your home back. But will I see you again?"

The unicorn said, "Carmen, you can depend on me. After all, we are friends."

Then the unicorn flew Carmen home. Again she was just in time for dinner.

Think About It

1. Tell how the unicorn's home looked before and after Carmen's visit.
2. How did Carmen help the unicorn and the other animals?
3. What did Carmen have in her emergency kit?
4. How did Carmen's imagination help her make Tragg disappear?
5. Make up another adventure with Carmen and the unicorn. Write it down, and share it with your friends.

Solve a Story Problem

In "Unicorn Days," Carmen must solve the problem caused by Tragg's bad magic. Many stories tell how people or animals solve a problem. Read this story, and then answer the questions that follow it.

On Wednesdays, Ned liked to do his homework after school and then play ball. But his sister Judy liked to play her flute first and then do her homework. Judy's flute was too loud, so Ned could not do his homework.

Ned had a good idea. If Judy did *her* homework when he did *his* homework, then she could play the flute while he played ball.

What problem did Ned and Judy have? How could they solve the problem?

Read about the book *Ducks Look the Same*, and answer the questions that follow.

Ducks Look the Same is a make-believe tale about a family of ducks. They swim happily on their lake, watching their reflections and looking for food.

But one day, a big fish begins to chase them. The ducks are afraid, so they borrow fifteen wooden ducks from a nearby farm and put them on the lake. The big fish catches a wooden duck. When it finds its mouth full of wood, it decides that ducks are not satisfying to eat after all.

What problem did the ducks have? How did they solve the problem?

Imagine That!

by ELIOT ROSS

The blue whale is the largest animal in the ocean. In fact, it is the largest animal on the earth. It is bigger than 30 elephants.

Even at an early age, the blue whale is huge. When born, it weighs more than seven elephants and is about 24 feet long, which makes the blue whale the world's biggest baby. Imagine that!

Sometimes you are barely able to imagine a strange fact, even if you know it is true. Try to imagine the strange-but-true facts on these pages.

Lightning strikes the earth hundreds and hundreds of times in a single minute. At any one time, there are many hundreds of storms coming down on the earth.

The air that blankets the earth is 600 miles deep.

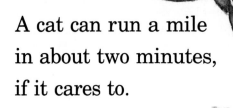

A cat can run a mile in about two minutes, if it cares to.

The world's thickest tree is
more than 100 feet around.

Light from the sun takes eight minutes
to reach the earth on a clear day or even
on a cloudy day.

The world's deepest hole made
by people is a huge well in
Oklahoma that goes down
more than five miles
into the earth.

It is often hard to imagine why people bother to do the things they do. Still, it is always fun to read about them.

Otto E. Funk journeyed on foot across the United States from New York City to San Francisco, playing merry music every step of the way.

It seemed endless to her listeners when Mary Davis talked for over 100 hours.

Thomas P. Hunt "walked" 56 yards, or 168 feet, on his hands in just over 18 seconds.

Maureen Weston rocked in a rocking chair for 432 hours.

Imagine that!

READ ON!

Worthington Botts and the Steam Machine by Betty Baker. Worthington Botts builds a machine that will do his jobs while he reads. How do things work out? Read to find out.

Keep Running, Allen! by Clyde Robert Bulla. Allen couldn't keep up with his sister and his two brothers. Read what happens one day when his sister and his brothers come looking for him.

Christina Katerina and the Box by Patricia Lee Gauch. Christina finds many uses for an old box.

Come Away by Myra Cohn Livingston. Alice and Mark visit many exciting places. Read this story to find out what happens to them.

UNIT 6

Blueprints

LEARN NEW WORDS

1. What is in the **center** of the park?
2. My **cousin** seems like a brother to me.
3. My **grandmother** arrived at one o'clock.
4. We rode the **monorail** around the park.
5. **Pioneer** houses tell us about the past.
6. We **searched** the woods for wild foxes.
7. What do these **symbols** stand for?
8. My **uncle** made a statue for my cousin.
9. That **amusement** park has many familiar rides.
10. My **aunt** visited us last Wednesday.
11. The **design** of the building pleased us.
12. She **explored** the park with her uncle.
13. Plant the bushes to make a **figure** eight.

GET SET TO READ

Losing your way is not fun!

Read to find out how Elaine uses a map to find her way.

Lost and Found

by FELIX MARQUARDT

I will never forget last Wednesday. I learned how to read a map for the first time. It was also the day Uncle Bradley and I almost got lost in Old America.

Everything started when my grandmother came to visit from Iowa and we were showing her around. We all decided to go to Old America. That's an amusement park that shows what the old days were like. It has wild animals, such as deer and foxes. There are pioneer houses where people do such things as carve wood toys or make cornmeal into bread. Old America has a Flatboat River Ride and a merry-go-round that is over one hundred years old. There is also a monorail that makes stops all around the park. You can look down from the monorail and see the whole park below.

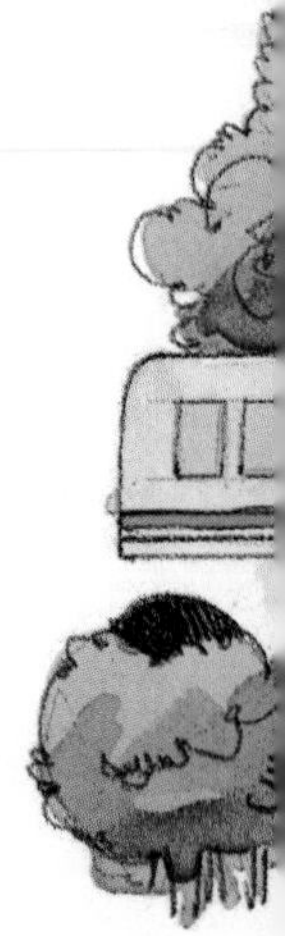

When we reached Old America, we were given a map. We spread it out. Grandma held one end, and my aunt held the other. We saw that the park wound in a design like a figure eight. The pioneer houses were built around the bottom part of the eight. The foxes were found at the top of the eight. The merry-go-round was set in the center of the design.

Grandma, Cousin Jeff, and Aunt Alice wanted to see the pioneer houses first. I really wanted to see the foxes. So my uncle said, "Elaine, let your aunt, your grandmother, and your cousin go where they want in the amusement park."

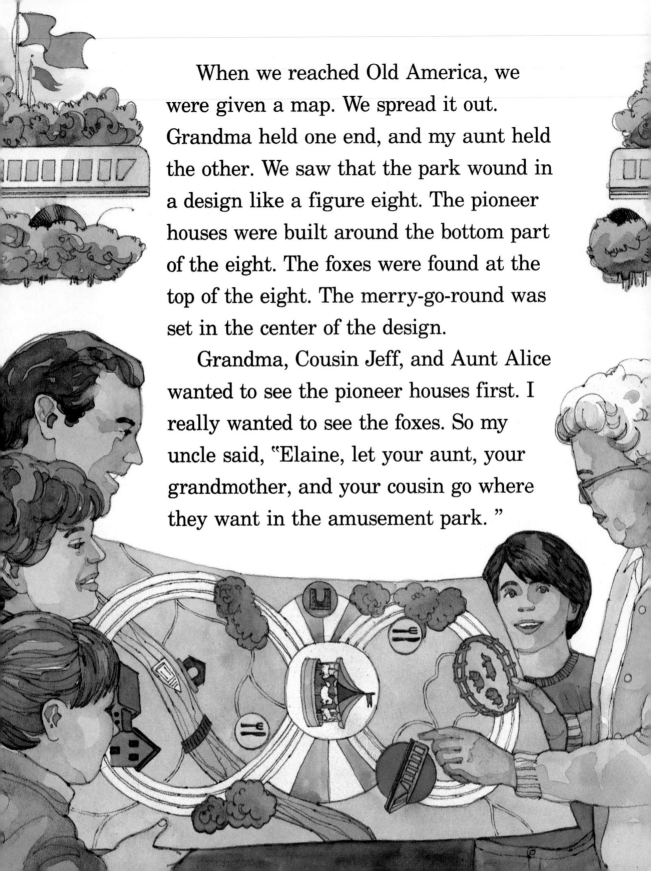

He added, "You and I will go by ourselves to see the foxes. We will all meet at the center of the amusement park by the merry-go-round at one o'clock."

Uncle Bradley and I set off in one direction. My aunt, my grandmother, and my cousin went in the other direction. My uncle and I explored the trails in the park and found the foxes. Then we explored the deer trail. I saw two deer!

Soon it was almost a quarter of one, so we decided to hurry to the merry-go-round in the center of the figure eight.

"Uncle Bradley, why didn't we take the map?" I asked. "Did you forget it?"

"Elaine, it should be easy to find the center of the amusement park," he said. "So I didn't think we would need a map."

Uncle Bradley and I walked until we came to a pioneer house where people were making meal from corn. The meal is used to make cornbread.

I told my uncle I thought we were lost, and he said, "You're right, Elaine. We must have missed the merry-go-round. Let's try going north."

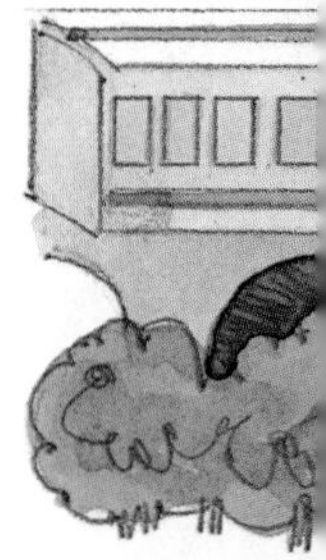

We searched a bit farther and came to where we thought the merry-go-round would be, but we did not see a single painted horse.

"This figure-eight design has me all mixed up," said Uncle Bradley. "It seems as if we're wandering around in circles."

"We're wandering around in figure eights!" I said.

I was afraid I was going to miss the merry-go-round. Just then, I noticed a big map on the side of one of the pioneer houses. I ran over to look at it.

There was a cross-shaped mark on the map. Under the cross-shaped mark were written the words, "You are here."

"Here we are, Uncle Bradley!" I said excitedly. Then I looked at all the symbols on the map and found the symbol for the merry-go-round.

"Look, Uncle Bradley!" I yelled. "There's the merry-go-round, and there is the symbol for the monorail station. We can take the monorail."

My uncle got out his glasses and searched the map. "You're right!" he said in a surprised voice.

"Well, what are we waiting for? Let's get to the station," I said.

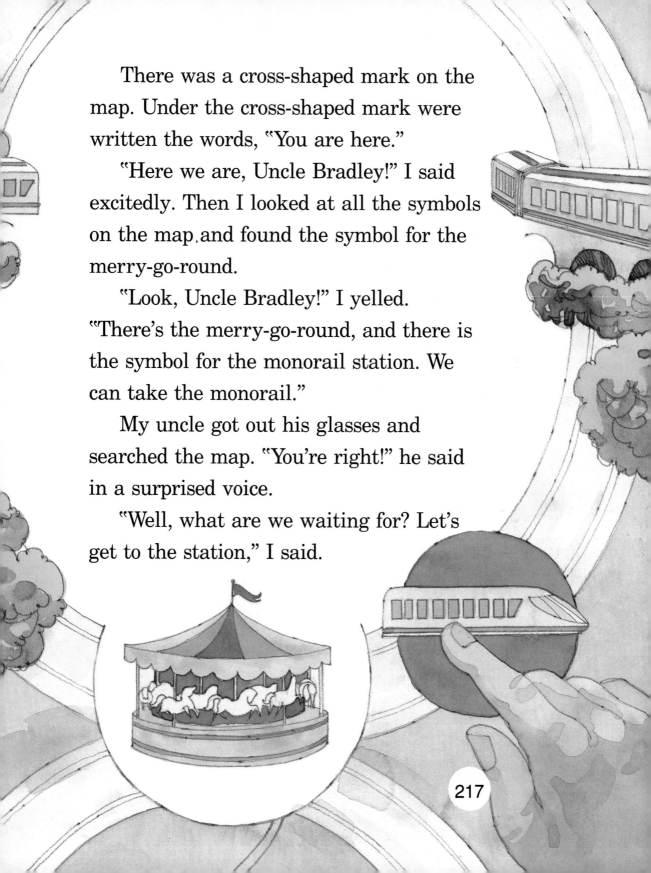

It was easy to find the monorail once we knew where to look. Soon we were high up on the train, looking at the park below us. We spotted my cousin, my aunt, and my grandmother waiting for us at the merry-go-round. Our search was over.

So that is how I learned to read a map. I guess you might say that I did it while doing a figure eight.

Think About It

1. Why did the family go different ways?
2. How did Elaine and her uncle plan to get around the amusement park?
3. How did the pioneer house map help?
4. How might Elaine have found her way without the map?
5. Design a make-believe amusement park. Tell about things you might have in it.

LEARN NEW WORDS

1. Mark the southern **boundaries** on this map.
2. What is the **capital** city of your state?
3. I'd like to meet a **famous** movie star.
4. He is an **important** man in our city.
5. The **manager** got all the work done.
6. Write down the **measurements** of the gym.
7. She was a famous stage **performer**.
8. He **studied** hard for the class.
9. **Thousands** of people enjoy baseball.
10. We heard beautiful music at the **opera**.
11. I hear merry tunes on the **radio** show.
12. A doctor must learn about **science**.

GET SET TO READ

Do you ever have to make plans before doing something?

Read to find out about two people who became great planners.

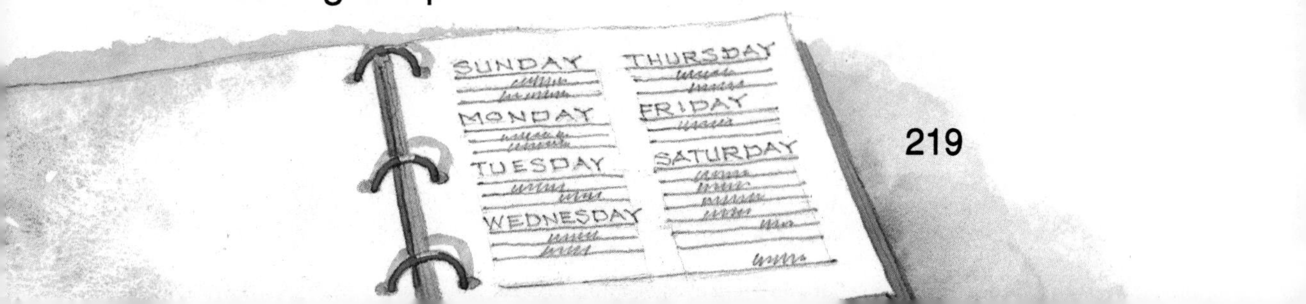

THE PLANNERS

by VALERIE GRANT

Chapter One: BENJAMIN BANNEKER

When you watch a play or visit a famous place, you may not realize that many people worked a long time on plans to put these things together.

What kinds of people do you suppose take part in the planning of great things? Well, they are people just like you and me. They use ideas to put together things that thousands of others can use or enjoy.

Benjamin Banneker is a person who didn't start out to be a great planner. But one day, he found himself taking part in the planning of our capital city, Washington, D.C. How did this happen?

Benjamin Banneker was born in Maryland in 1731. When he was a young boy, his parents needed Benjamin to help work on their farm. He barely had time to go to school. But he was interested in many different things. So he studied on his own and taught himself math and science.

Benjamin's neighbors, George and Andrew Ellicott, were interested in *astronomy*, a science about the sun, the moon, and the stars. They taught young Benjamin as much as they knew about that science. Then they helped him find more books to study all the things he was interested in learning. They also thought he should write little books about the weather to help farmers plan their work.

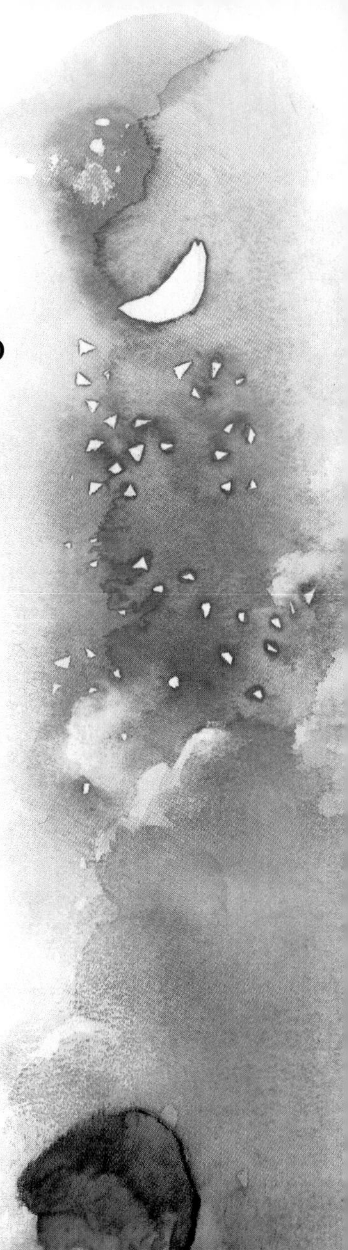

Benjamin was very happy working on his books. But in 1791, he began to work on an important job with Andrew Ellicott.

Andrew was a surveyor. A *surveyor* is a person who takes measurements of land so that streets and cities can be built. Andrew knew that Benjamin was very good in math and science. He needed someone to help him take measurements and plan the boundaries for the new capital of our country. The capital was to be named Washington after George Washington.

Pierre L'Enfant, a man from France, made drawings of how the new city would be laid out. It was planned around two center squares. In one square would be the Capitol. The streets would branch out from both squares in all directions, like lines from the center of a wheel. The design wound up being both beautiful and different.

Benjamin and Andrew worked hard as they laid out boundaries in all directions. But work suddenly stopped when Pierre L'Enfant became angry with the way the work was going. He left for France, and everyone was afraid the planning would have to start all over.

But Benjamin knew the plans very well, so he was able to help redo the map of the city. Benjamin and Andrew worked together to finish the job. Benjamin had become a very important planner of one of the most beautiful capital cities in the world.

Chapter Two: BEVERLY SILLS

Another famous planner also did not start out to be one. At first, she was only interested in being a performer.

Today, Beverly Sills is the manager of the New York City Opera, even though she was a starring opera singer for many years.

Like a play, an opera tells a story. But instead of speaking lines, the players sing the words of the story.

Beverly always wanted to perform on the stage. She wanted to wear fine costumes, sing beautiful songs, and be an important part of the many wonderful operas that people would see and enjoy.

At the age of three, she performed in front of many people for the first time. She was heard on radio shows. So many people loved listening to these radio shows that Beverly became a child star.

But there are not many parts for child performers in opera. Beverly had to wait until she was older before she could begin to sing opera. She knew it would take many years to train her voice and study opera. So she began the special voice lessons needed to become an opera singer.

Beverly studied and waited until after she finished high school. Then she joined a small opera company. Soon more and more people were beginning to notice her beautiful voice.

At last, she was asked to join the New York City Opera, one of the finest opera companies in the world.

During the years she performed with the company, Beverly brought joy to thousands and thousands of people with her beautiful singing. She became world famous.

Then the time came when she decided to stop being a performer. Many people did not want her to leave opera. Beverly, too, wanted to stay close to opera in some way. So when she was asked to manage the company and plan future operas, she said yes. Now she was a planner instead of a performer. As manager, she would have an even more important part in bringing exciting operas to music lovers.

As the manager of the New York City Opera, Beverly must make sure that the music, singing, lighting, costumes, dancing, and sets are just right.

Beverly works every day planning the operas her company performs. She is busier now as a planner and a manager than she ever was as a famous singer.

Think About It

1. What planners did you read about?
2. How did Beverly Sills's early years help her become a good opera planner?
3. How was Beverly Sills's schooling different from Benjamin Banneker's?
4. What is different about the plans Benjamin Banneker made and the plans Beverly Sills makes?
5. What are other things that need planning?

Did It Really Happen?

The stories you have read about Benjamin Banneker and Beverly Sills are called **nonfiction** because they are true. "Lost and Found" is not true. It is called **fiction.**

How can you tell if a story is nonfiction or fiction? Some clues can help you. Clues in fiction can be make-believe people, times, places, or things that could or could not have happened. Nonfiction tells true facts about real people, times, places, and things.

Read the sentences and answer the questions.

1. The singer Marian Anderson was born in 1902.

2. Tom met a jealous dragon in the forest.

Which sentence is nonfiction? Which is fiction? What clues helped you decide?

Read these two stories and tell which is fiction and which is nonfiction. What clues helped you decide?

1. In 1527, a tall, dark-skinned African named Estevanico sailed to Florida with a group of Spanish sailors. Estevanico went exploring as far as what we now call Arizona. Many tales were told about him by different groups of Indians who were happy to share their homes with him.
2. There was a tiny, magical moose named Hoot who lived in the desert. He could sing like an opera star and play merry music. For fun, he usually carved wooden geese with a sharp knife. In school, he even got straight *A*'s in science and math!

LEARN NEW WORDS

1. I like the way these **biscuits** taste.
2. The cowhands made a big circle and rounded up all the **cattle**.
3. He gave Davy a **nudge** to wake him.
4. His horse **plunged** into the icy water.
5. The dry branches **rattled** in the wind.
6. The **steer** was taken into the barn.
7. The horse **stumbled** over the bundles of wood.

GET SET TO READ

When you do something for the first time, do you ever feel both excited and afraid?

As you read, see how Davy feels about his first trail drive.

OLD BLUE

adapted from a story
by SIBYL HANCOCK

"Wake up, Davy!"

Davy opened his eyes and saw Cookie standing over him. "I'll be right there." Davy groaned and pushed off his blanket. Most of the cowhands would soon be getting up to eat breakfast. The ones who had been out all night watching the cattle would be coming in.

Davy was rubbing his eyes when he felt a familiar nudge. He looked up and saw a huge longhorn steer with a hide so coal black it looked nearly blue.

"Old Blue," Davy said softly. "Are you hungry and thirsty, too, old fellow?"

Davy rubbed Old Blue's head and said, "You're the smartest old steer the ranch ever had." Old Blue was the leader of the cattle herd on the trail drive.

At breakfast, Davy told Cookie, "Pa said I can ride with the cowhands today!"

"You're a lucky fellow, son. I guess not many young fellows get to go on a trail ride," Cookie said. "But right now, we have important work to do here. The cowhands are very hungry." Cookie handed Davy a plate of biscuits, corn, and stew.

As the cowhands chewed their biscuits, Davy brought some food scraps to Old Blue. Pa met him there and whistled for a saddle horse for Davy to ride.

"Let's get moving," Pa said.

Davy climbed on his horse and followed Old Blue up to the head of the moving herd.

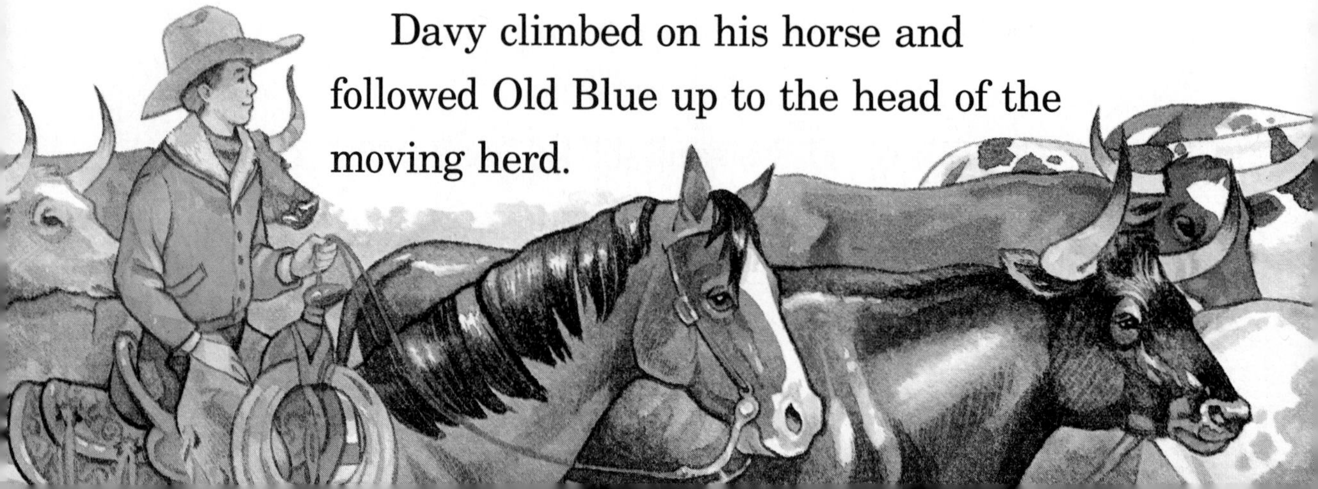

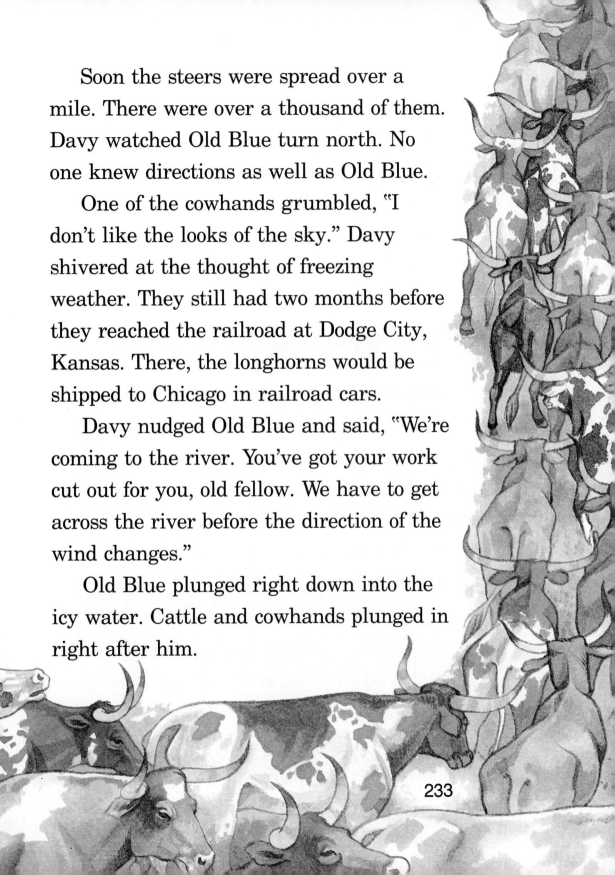

Soon the steers were spread over a mile. There were over a thousand of them. Davy watched Old Blue turn north. No one knew directions as well as Old Blue.

One of the cowhands grumbled, "I don't like the looks of the sky." Davy shivered at the thought of freezing weather. They still had two months before they reached the railroad at Dodge City, Kansas. There, the longhorns would be shipped to Chicago in railroad cars.

Davy nudged Old Blue and said, "We're coming to the river. You've got your work cut out for you, old fellow. We have to get across the river before the direction of the wind changes."

Old Blue plunged right down into the icy water. Cattle and cowhands plunged in right after him.

The cold water splashed onto Davy's face. He huddled under his coat as his horse stumbled, plunged, and then began to swim to the shore on the other side. It took a long time for the herd to reach the shore.

By afternoon, the sky grew dark. A streak of lightning flashed. Thunder boomed. Horns rattled together, and thousands of hooves pounded the dirt. Some of the cattle stumbled, and the rattling grew louder.

"Stampede!" Pa cried.

Davy rode his horse away from the cattle. Then he watched the cowhands lead Old Blue around in a circle. The herd of cattle followed and soon wound up running in a huge circle. This was called *milling,* and it was the only way to stop a stampede.

The air burst with electricity. Davy could see ghostly sparks dancing on the edge of his hat and around his horse's ears. He even saw sparks on the tips of the cattle's horns.

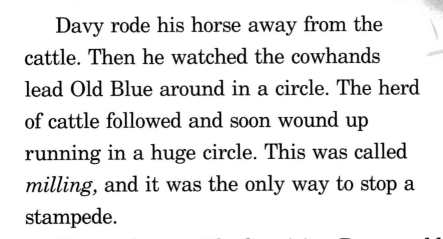

When the herd settled down, Davy rode silently back to camp. He found Cookie by the chuck wagon building a fire. "It's going to be a bad night," Cookie said. Davy felt the wind grow colder.

Pa rode up to the wagon. "We need every cowhand to saddle up now," he said. "We can't let the cattle stampede again. I can use your help, too, Davy."

Davy pulled his hat lower and plunged in to work with the other cowhands.

Before midnight, the rain turned to sleet. Davy heard someone singing in the darkness to keep the cattle quiet.

Then the sleet turned to snow. Davy couldn't even see Old Blue. It was the worst night he could ever remember.

In the morning, the worst of the storm was over. Everyone took turns eating and standing by the fire to get warm.

"Do you want to ride in the chuck wagon?" Pa asked Davy.

Davy shook his head no.

Pa said, "You're doing fine, son." Then he asked Cookie, "How do you keep a fire burning in this snow?"

"That's my secret," Cookie said.

Suddenly Old Blue came up and nudged Davy gently for a bite of his biscuit.

"I almost lost you last night, old fellow," Davy said to the steer. "When we get back to the ranch, I am going to buy you a bell to wear around your neck. Then we will always know where you are."

"It's a good idea if it works," Pa said. "No person has ever belled a lead steer. But no steer was ever as tame as Old Blue."

"I've got a bell in the wagon," Cookie said. He held up a brass bell and a rope.

Davy gently placed the bell around Old Blue's neck. Old Blue shook his horns and listened to the bell clang.

"Look how proud that old steer is," said Pa with a laugh. "He must think that bell is a prize!"

If a longhorn could smile, Old Blue would have.

Think About It

1. What did Davy do on the trail that was both exciting and scary?
2. Why do you think Old Blue was placed at the front of the herd?
3. Why did Davy hang a bell around Old Blue's neck?
4. What are some of the things you would have to think about if you were planning a cattle drive?
5. Write a story about what you might see and hear if you camped out on a cattle drive.

Blue Monday

by AMALIA SPIEGEL

That Monday, huge dark clouds were throwing great shadows over everything. It looked as if a storm were about to begin any minute. Miss Loloma said to the class, "Let's choose a bouncy song to sing to cheer ourselves up on this blue, blue Monday."

Miguel raised his hand and asked, "What is a *blue Monday,* anyway?"

Miss Loloma said, "Many people are sad on Monday because the weekend is over. Many people think that blue is a sad color, too."

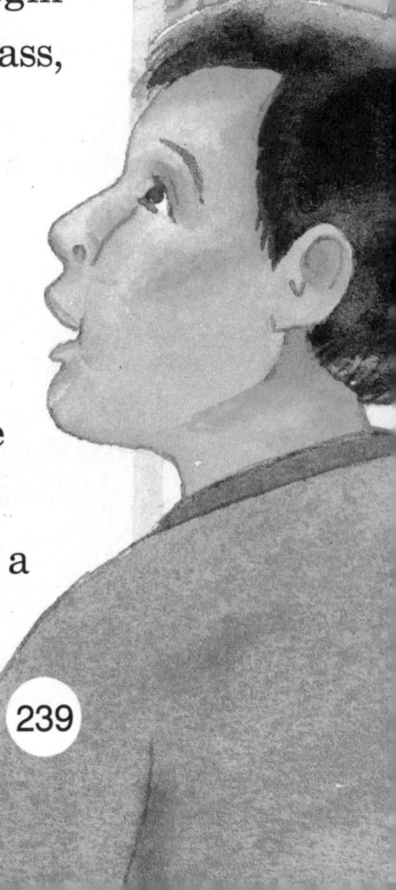

Miguel didn't like that at all and said, "Blue makes me happy, not sad. When the sky is blue, it means the sun is out, and nothing is better than a blue sky."

Most of the children in the class felt as Miguel did, so Miss Loloma said, "Why don't we have a *happy* blue Monday? Next Monday, we'll all wear or bring something blue to school."

Everyone liked this idea, except Rita, who said, "What's so wonderful about blue? My favorite color is orange, so I want to bring in something orange and have an *orange* Monday."

Miguel said, "You had better bring in something blue. Everyone has to!"

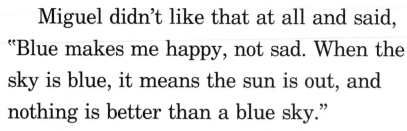

"All right, then," said Rita, "I'll bring in a blue rose."

"There's no such thing," grumbled Miguel.

"She must mean a paper rose," said Elena.

"No, I mean a real blue rose," said Rita, "and if I bring one to class, may we have an orange Monday the next week?"

"That sounds fair," said Miss Loloma. "If you bring something as special as a blue rose, we'll have an orange Monday."

"It will never happen in a million years," said Miguel.

But Rita smiled and said, "You should start thinking of something orange to bring to class."

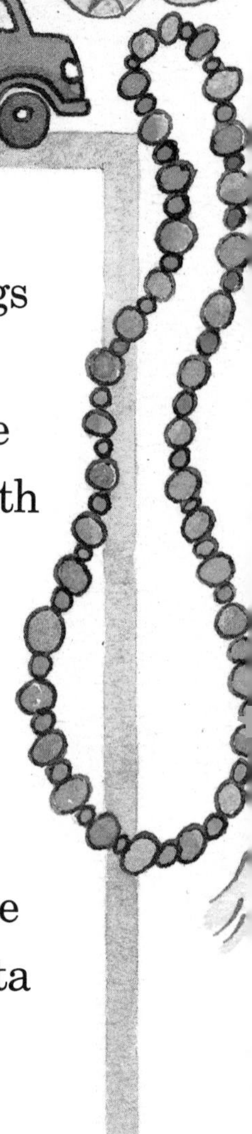

The next Monday, everyone came to class wearing or carrying the blue things they had collected.

Miss Loloma had on a blue cape. She also brought a small bear made of smooth blue stone. Miguel had a bluebird's feather sticking in his hat. Elena had brought blue clay for people to make things with. There were blue marbles, blue whistles, blue trucks, and blue toy turtles. It was fun looking at all the blue things, but everyone was waiting for Rita and her blue rose.

"We might have a long, long wait," said Miguel, and everyone giggled.

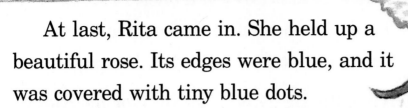

At last, Rita came in. She held up a beautiful rose. Its edges were blue, and it was covered with tiny blue dots.

"Where did you get it?" asked Elena.

"Anyone can change the color of a flower," said Rita. "All I did was add blue food coloring to water and put a white rose in it. The rose soaked up the blue color with the water."

"The flower did the work," said Paul.

"It's so beautiful," said Cindy.

"I'm going to try it," said Elena.

Miguel didn't say anything.

"What's the matter, Miguel?" asked Miss Loloma.

"I'm thinking," said Miguel.

"About what?" asked Elena.

Miguel laughed and said, "About what to bring in for our orange Monday."

READ ON!

Louie's Search by Ezra Jack Keats. Louie has a plan to find someone. Read this story to find out what happens.

Girls Can Be Anything by Norma Klein. Girls can plan to be whatever they want to be. Read to find out some of the things that girls can be.

The Mysterious Prowler by Joan Lowery Nixon. Jonathan tries to find the person who has been ringing the doorbell and calling on the telephone. Read to find out how Jonathan finds clues to solve the case.

Arthur Mitchell: Dancer by Tobi Tobias. Read the story of Arthur Mitchell, one of America's leading dancers.

GLOSSARY

A

a · ble She was *able* to put all of her old toys and games in two boxes.

a · bove The birds were flying just *above* the water.

ad · ven · ture Finding a cave filled with gold was an exciting *adventure*.

a · gainst He put his nose *against* the window.

a · head The car *ahead* of them stopped.

al · li · ga · tors *Alligators* live where it is hot and damp.

a · muse · ment We had a good time at the *amusement* park.

ap · pear All at once, I saw a boat *appear* on the lake.

ar · rived He *arrived* at the party on time.

aunt My *aunt* looks like my mother.

au · tumn The hare sniffed the cool *autumn* air.

a · wake She was *awake* when I went into her room.

B

be · came The weather *became* cloudy in the afternoon.

be · gan I *began* to get sleepy after my bath.

be · gins The story *begins* when Caleb joins the circus.

be • long Does this sack *belong* to you?

be • low The chairs were *below* the window.

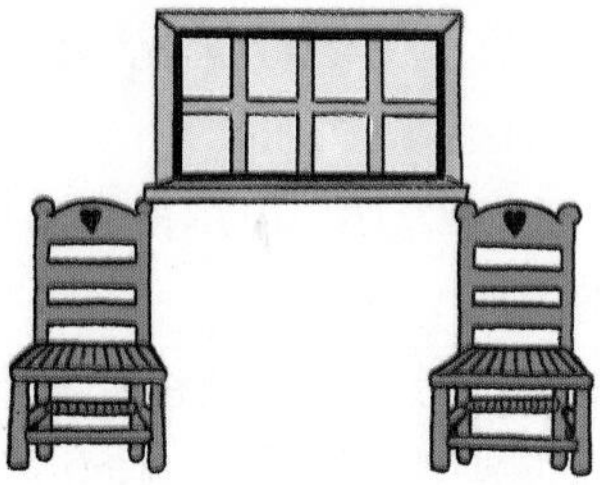

be • sides There are many things to eat *besides* eggs.

be • yond The top shelf is *beyond* my reach.

bis • cuits I like hot *biscuits* with cold milk.

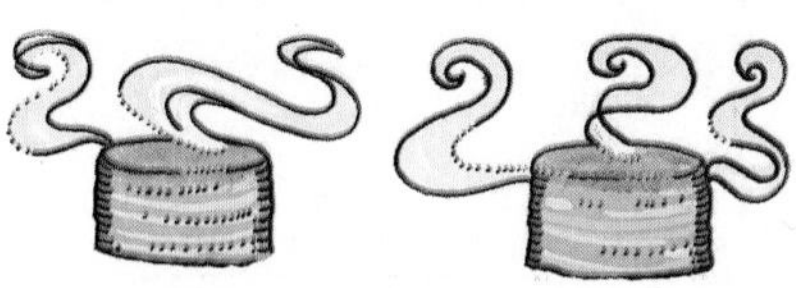

blan • ket The *blanket* on my bed keeps me warm.

bot • tom There was a light at the *bottom* of the stairs.

bound • a • ries The city's *boundaries,* or edges, are clearly marked on the map.

break • fast I eat a good *breakfast* every morning.

built The girl *built* a house from blocks of wood.

burn • ing The fire was *burning* for a long time.

but • ter I put some melted *butter* on a roll.

C

cap • i • tal We visited the *capital* city of Texas.

cat • tle Davy helped lead the *cattle* to the barn.

cel • lo I am learning to play a new tune on my *cello.*

cen · ter He put the table in the *center* of the room.

chew Did the dog *chew* on a stick?

clear · ing We camped in a *clearing* in the woods.

clue I need a *clue* to help me find the answer to the problem.

col · lect · ed She *collected* stamps from around the world.

cork The *cork* will keep air from getting into the jar.

course Of *course* you can go!

cous · in I will stay with my *cousin* all summer.

D

dark · ness We could not see the sign in the *darkness*.

de · pends She *depends* on me to help her with her work.

de · sign I like the *design* on your clothes.

di · rect Don't circle around; take the most *direct* path.

di · rec · tion He walked in the *direction* of his house.

dis · ap · peared The setting sun *disappeared* behind the mountain.

dom · i · noes We play a game of *dominoes* every night.

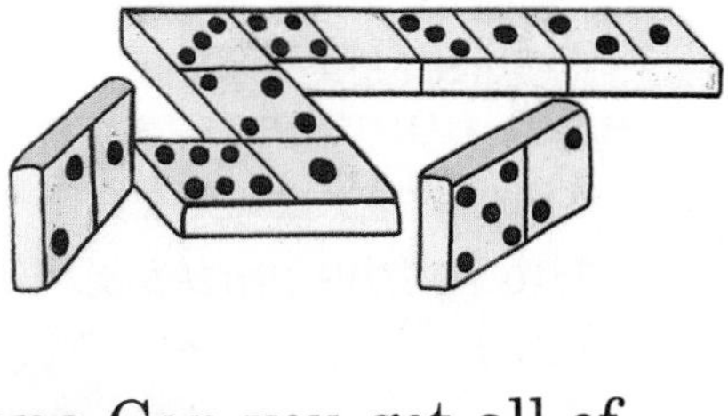

done Can you get all of your work *done* today?

drag · ons Do *dragons* really make fire?

dur · ing We did not stand up *during* the game.

E

ea · gle The *eagle* has large, strong wings.

earth The farmers planted vegetables in the *earth.*

ei · ther I will buy *either* this suit or that suit.

e · lec · tric · i · ty We couldn't turn the lights on because the *electricity* was cut off.

e · mer · gen · cy In case of an *emergency,* call this special number.

end · less This river is so long it seems *endless.*

en · er · gy *Energy* from the sun can heat our homes.

es · capes If doors are blocked, leave by the fire *escapes.*

eve · ning In the *evening,* we have dinner and read.

ex · act · ly His answer was *exactly* right.

ex · er · cis · es Our *exercises* help keep us strong.

ex · plored The campers *explored* the old cave.

ex · tra After I gave one to Dad, I had two *extra* apples.

F

fa · mil · iar This *familiar* town is where I grew up.

fa · mous We wanted to meet the *famous* baseball player.

far · ther She walks much *farther* to school than I.

fa · vor Doing a *favor* for you always makes me feel good.

few There are only a *few* leaves left on the tree.

fig · ure She drew the *figure* of a cat.

fi · nal · ly We *finally* made it home after our trip.

fish · er · man Did the *fisherman* catch any fish?

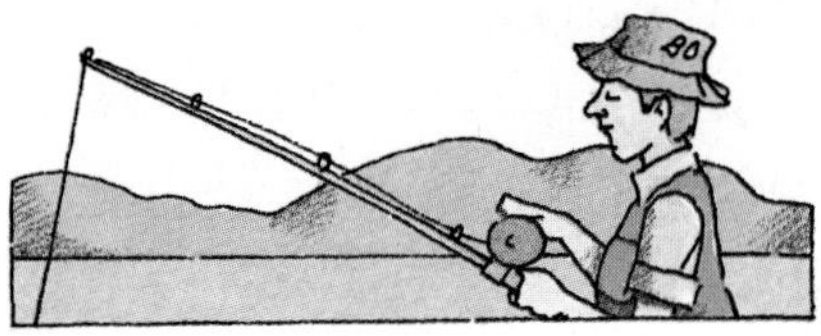

flew A bat *flew* past my head.

for · get Don't *forget* to bring your books home after school.

full I need a *full* pail of water for the plants.

fu · ture In the *future,* this puppy will become a big dog.

G

gen · tly Touch the baby *gently,* or he will cry.

ghost · ly A *ghostly* sound made us shiver in the darkness.

gig · gles Pat *giggles* when I tell funny stories.

grand · moth · er *Grandmother* and Grandfather visited us.

guess Can you *guess* the answer to the riddle?

H

ham · mock The child rested in a *hammock* hung between two tall trees.

horn Hold the goat by its left *horn.*

hour It took one *hour* to get home.

hud · dle If we *huddle* together, there will be room for us all.

I

I'm *I'm* happy that you came to the party.

im · por · tant I forgot to give you an *important* message.

in · ter · est · ed I am *interested* in what you have to say.

is · land We took a boat ride around the *island*.

J

jack · et Her winter *jacket* kept her warm.

jeal · ous I was *jealous* of Bob's baseball cap because it was newer than mine.

jour · neyed They *journeyed* to a new land.

jun · gle Unusual birds and animals live in a *jungle*.

L

lies My cat often *lies* in the sun to sleep.

li · on We heard a *lion* roar at the zoo.

lum · ber The builder needed more *lumber* to finish the house.

M

mag · i · cal I flew to a *magical* land behind the moon.

make-be · lieve My little sister made a *make-believe* house from a big box.

man · ag · er The *manager* made sure the work was done.

mar · bles The green ones are my favorite *marbles*.

mat · ter Does it *matter* if I wear a blue tie or a green tie?

meas · ure · ments We need the *measurements* of the room before starting the work.

mer · ry The boy was bright and *merry*.

mes · sage Please leave her a *message* to call me on the telephone.

mid · dle Fold your paper down the *middle*.

mil · lions There are *millions* of fish in the sea.

min · ute It took me one *minute* to get here.

mir · ror I saw my face in the *mirror*.

mo · ment It will only take me a *moment* to finish the work.

Mon · day *Monday* is the first day of the week at school.

mon · o · rail From the car on the *monorail*, we could see the zoo below us.

months How many more *months* until your birthday?

N

near I live *near* the lake.

neigh · bors All of my *neighbors* are nice people.

north The baseball field is *north* of town.

no · tice She did not *notice* that the clock had stopped.

nudge The horse gave the girl a *nudge* when it was hungry.

nu · mer · als It was hard to see the *numerals* on the grandfather clock.

O

o · cean Big waves make it hard to swim in the *ocean.*

o'clock The movie will start at two *o'clock.*

of · fered Mom *offered* to drive us to school.

op · er · a We enjoyed the music we heard at the *opera.*

P

palm A colorful bird sat on top of the *palm* tree.

peb · ble She had a *pebble* stuck in her shoe.

per · form · er I clapped when the *performer* finished singing.

per · haps *Perhaps* they won't go, but maybe they will.

per · son Are you the *person* who wrote this letter?

pi · o · neer The *pioneer* houses showed us how people used to live.

plunged The happy children *plunged* into the water.

pow · er That train needs a lot of *power* to run.

pre · cious The famous painting is as *precious* as gold.

pre · tend · ed We each *pretended* to be a different animal.

pud · dles After it rained, there were *puddles* of water in the street.

Q

quar · ter The four of us each ate a *quarter* of the apple.

R

ra · di · o We turned on the *radio* and danced to the music.

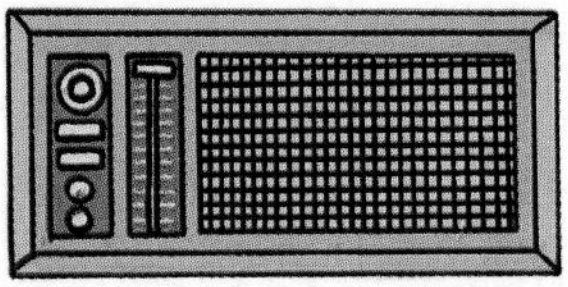

rat · tled The old window banged and *rattled* in the wind.

re · al · ized Jody *realized* that she didn't know the answer.

re · flec · tion He looked in the lake and saw his *reflection.*

re · fused They *refused* to offer us any help.

re · mind · ed She *reminded* me to give the dog a bath.

re · turned We *returned* home after our trip to the lake.

rid · dle Do you know the answer to this *riddle*?

riv · er We floated across the *river* on a raft.

ru · ined The heavy rain *ruined* the garden.

S

sad · dle After riding, she took the *saddle* off the horse.

safe · ty They weren't afraid in the *safety* of their home.

sci · ence I learn about living things in *science.*

searched We *searched* the paper for news of the fire.

sea · shore We looked for shells by the *seashore.*

sec · onds She won the race by three *seconds.*

sen · tenc · es Pete was writing *sentences* for his story.

shim · mer · ing The king's *shimmering* coat of gold was as bright as the sunshine.

shiv · er · ing The small dog was *shivering* in the cold wind.

sign I didn't see the stop *sign.*

si · lent The children were *silent* as the teacher spoke.

sil · ver Dad brushed *silver* paint on my bicycle.

sin · gle There wasn't a *single* piece of food left on the table.

six · ty In *sixty* days it will be my birthday.

slip · pers My *slippers* were under the bed.

soared The plane *soared* into the sky.

so · lar We get *solar* energy from the sun.

solve My teacher helped me *solve* the problem.

son The father took his *son* by the hand.

spar · rows The *sparrows* have brown and gray wings.

sta · tion The space *station* will help us find out about other planets.

stat · ues We made clay *statues* in art class.

steer The *steer* shook its horns and stamped its hooves.

store We bought new shoes at the *store.*

storm The *storm* brought lots of wind and rain.

straight Amy walked *straight* through my yard to her house.

strength Using all of her *strength,* she was able to pick up the heavy box.

stud · ied I have *studied* music for three years.

stum · bled As I was hurrying to dress, I *stumbled* over my shoes on the floor.

sup · pose I *suppose* I should tell her today.

swapped We *swapped* a balloon for a bag of peanuts.

swept The bird *swept* low over the scared rabbit.

sym·bols The red circles on the map are the *symbols* for fire stations.

T

tears There were *tears* in my eyes because the wind was blowing so hard.

thirst · y The *thirsty* children drank their milk quickly.

thou · sands The sky was filled with *thousands* of stars.

thun · der We heard *thunder,* and then it began to rain.

ti · ny I could hardly see the *tiny* dot on the paper.

to · ward The bus was going *toward* my house.

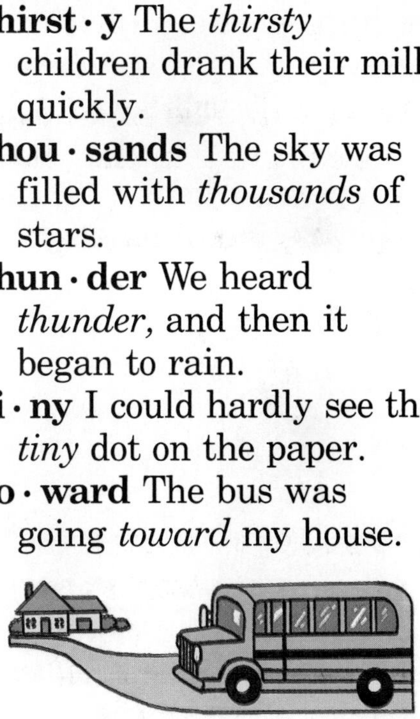

tow · er The old bell hung in the *tower* on top of the building.

tunes Bob *tunes* his banjo so he can play nice music.

tur · tles *Turtles* can live in water or on land.

twelve There were *twelve* children at my party.

U

un · cle I was happy to get a letter from my *uncle.*

un · hap · pi · ness I felt great *unhappiness* when my best friend moved away.

u · ni · corns The make-believe animals I like best are *unicorns.*

W

wan · der Don't *wander* too far from the house.

washed The sea *washed* over the rocks.

wear I would like to *wear* my new dress.

Wednes · day *Wednesday* is in the middle of the week.

wound · ed The doctor took care of the *wounded* man.

writ · ten Have you *written* a letter to Alice yet?

Y

young Her son is too *young* to drive.